Eliza Ann Woodruff Hopkins

Little Shells from many Shores

Eliza Ann Woodruff Hopkins

Little Shells from many Shores

ISBN/EAN: 9783743302778

Manufactured in Europe, USA, Canada, Australia, Japa

Cover: Foto ©Thomas Meinert / pixelio.de

Manufactured and distributed by brebook publishing software
(www.brebook.com)

Eliza Ann Woodruff Hopkins

Little Shells from many Shores

FROM

MANY SHORES.

BY

MRS. E. A. W. HOPKINS.

SAN FRANCISCO:

BACON & COMPANY, PRINTERS, EXCELSIOR OFFICE,

No. 536 Clay Street.

1872.

PREFACE.

A severe family affliction prevented the publication of this work in April—as I had promised you. Out of the delay, the increased necessity for economy, and difficulties which could not properly be explained on this page, has arisen the change of publishers.

The Poems contained in this volume are selections from manuscripts, old and new, and clippings of my own, from journals to which I have contributed for many years, in some half a dozen States and under a dozen signatures—"Mrs. C. B. H.," "E. A. W. H.," etc., etc.

In selecting for the book, I have remembered that my friends are persons of varied attainments and tastes; and while I aimed to please many, have hoped to offend none.

Perhaps the volume may not inaptly be compared to one of our California highways—with its big and little stones, its sticks and straws, old tin cans, and broken bottles; with here and there a tiny grain of gold. As it is, I commend it to your generosity.

AUTHORESS.

INDEX.

INDEX.

LITTLE SHELLS FROM MANY SHORES.

LITTLE SHELLS from many strands,
Bring I you with loving hands;
Rosy shells of pleasures fled—
Broken shells of hopes long dead,
Silvery shells of life's proud prime—
Tear-stained shells of later time,
Gathered with a smooth, young brow—
Gathered when as dark as now;
Looking back to long ago,
Forward through the falling snow,
Almost where the two worlds meet,
Lo! I lay them at your feet.

EVENING AND MORNING OF THE BATTLE

OF ANTIETAM.

"The hostile lines lay close to each other; their pickets so near that six rebels were captured during the night. The great battle commenced early next day."

A corn-field here, a wheat-field there,
A hill-side green and gray,
A graceful wood, a meadow fair,
A town, a public way;
A river spanned by bridges three,
Four miles of water, wood and lea,
In smiling sunset lay.

As cities in the far-off light,
Our vision doubts as real;
Now looming o'er the sea of white
With spires of glittering steel;

Now lost beneath a darkling wave,

Now rising from their shadow grave,

   Then gone, as all ideal.

As evening crossed with tempest bars

   A moment, then a glow,

And bursting with her myriad stars

   From heavy clouds below ;

Two armies rise, and fall, and pass ;

A surge of ink—a wave of glass—

   And melt away as snow.

One is the North ; resolved and stern,

   She spans those vales and steeps,

The lightnings of her anger burn,

   While love reluctant weeps ;

She hears to-morrow's dismal tramp,

Just o'er yon Orient's dark and damp,

   That counts her crimsoned heaps.

One is the South ; impassioned, wild,

   With hot and feverish breath ;

The friend estranged, the wayward child,
  That seeks her mother's death ;
With desperate threats and bloodshot eye,
And murmuring still her battle cry,
  She halts upon the heath.

Soft as a gentle mother's thrall,
  That all her babes entwines ;
Soft as the angel footsteps fall
  When day's bright orb declines ;
Came sleep, and showered leaves of balm
O'er North and South—her holy calm
  Encircling all their lines.

The white-lipped Morn rebukes the dark,
  And pensive smiles again ;
Ascending sings the early lark,
  And skims the upper main ;
Soft peeping through a clouding veil,
The sunbeams come, aslant and pale,
  And kiss the dew-gemmed plain.

Sons of the North !—sons of the South !

  As brothers, close ye slept;

The same tree-shadow touched ye both,

  As East at eve it crept ;

The same good angels watched ye there,

Then, lifting up for each a prayer,

  On Mercy's threshold wept.

Each silver thread that spans the blue,

  And trembles on the corn,

Rekindling all the hills anew,

  Salutes ye, " brothers born ;"

One father's own electric thrill

In all your veins, unites ye still,

  O hearts asunder torn !

How can ye wake to strike again,

  Or fan your bosom's hate ?

Why doom afresh to grief and pain

  One last night's sleeping mate ?

Oh ! by one country's lingering woes;

2

Oh ! by one Saviour's dying throes,
  We pray—we warn ye—wait !

As trickling drops of homestead wells
  When rise the buckets slow ;
Or murmuring bees in flowery dells,
  Is fair Antietam's flow.
But—hark ! a war note's dismal sound !
Air, earth and heaven at once rebound,
  And ring it to and fro.

It was, as if all fearful things
  In every dark retreat,
Had started up with flapping wings,
  And tramped with pond'rous feet ;
As if all discords, born of hell,
Condensed in one wild, thrilling yell,
  Kept time with heavy beat.

It was, as if all earthly power
  Had hardened into stone,

While hideous Murder ruled the hour,

   And laughed upon her throne ;

As if all Heaven looked down and smiled,

While human blood the earth defiled,

   And *shimmered in the sun !*

THE HERDSMEN'S "GOOD NIGHT!"

When 'mong the Alpine hills the sun
 Hath left the vales in shade below,
And glimmers like a jeweled crown
 Upon the arching cliffs of snow:

The herdsman of the loftiest height
 Takes up his horn, and shouts aloud :
" Praise God, the Lord !" and swift as light
 Comes echoing back, " Praise God—praise God !"

A hundred herdsmen catch the strain,
 And shout the words with horns anew ;
The rocks take up the loud refrain,
 And solemn caves repeat it too.

Along the hills the cadence steals,
 And quivers o'er unnumbered streams,

Till every heart the influence feels,
And nature's self hath holier dreams.

" Praise God, the Lord ! " O man of years,
For fearless heart, and tireless hand,
For gladsome hours, for sorrow's tears,
And faith to see the " better land."

" Praise Him," O maid, for beauty's blush ;
" Praise Him," O youth, for thou art strong ;
" Praise Him," O matron, for the hush
Of peace upon thy hearth so long.

" Praise Him," O child, for sky and flowers,
For verdant moss and clambering vines,
For love that guards thy mountain bowers,
And sets thy feet their boundary lines.

Lo ! deeper shadows climb the rocks,
And dewy night has set them there ;
Uncovered as their silent flocks,
They bow their heads in secret prayer.

All nature joins ; with reverent hush
   The mountain wind suspends her breath ;
Young leaves, that fluttered on the bush
   In ceaseless play, are still as death.

" Good-night ! " again the horns resound,
   And many a voice as one replies,
Till echo, circling round and round,
   In silvery cadence sweetly dies.

THE SILENT PASSENGER.

With its inanimate and living freight
The noisy train whirls on.

                    And happy hearts
Beat lightly as the buzzing wheels speed by
The meadows and the corn ; the orchard fair,
With all its goodly trees of blushing fruit,
Its foliage spinning ribbons as we fly,
Its fence a quivering cord ; the homestead meek,
Its windows muslin-draped and wreathed with vines.
The lazy house-dog, sleeping in the sun,
Upstarts a moment to his feet, with one
Deep, sonorous bark, and then two lesser notes,
And folds his limbs again.   The maid steals out,
With broom in hand and apron o'er her head,
To see this daily show, which comes and goes
As the cloud-shadow flitting o'er the grain,
As the loud thunder shaking all the plain.
And here the village, in its white and green,

Its lettered doors, its awnings, and its wealth
Of shawls and ginghams fluttering in the wind,
Comes smiling up to meet us in good haste;
The whistle shrill cuts sharply on the ear;
The brakeman's at his post; the ponderous wheels
Upon their axles turn with lessening speed,
And slowly cease to sound.   The school-boy stands
And counts the number of the graceless cars,
With sweet, blue eyes a-stare; the mountaineer,
Who for this sight alone has come to town,
Pushes his way along, exclaims and smiles.

Lo! what a crowd is gathering where we halt,
A pleasant show of faces, earnest all,
And glistening eyes which speak a "welcome home!"
Seek out the friends so dear—the new-arrived.
Hands meet in friendly clasp, and trembling lips
Give blessed recognition, murmuring low.

The walking groups move off; there, too, upspring
Light, joyous footsteps to the waiting seat
In the old family carriage—that is gone.

We, too, are happier, though we know them not.

For homes await in distance even us,

E'en us—poor travelers! we shall soon be there.

But see, as breaks the close and motley crowd,

Those wagons blocking up the village street.

Behold! that hearse with plumes of inky hue,

With solemn drapery and steeds of white.

It backs toward the train, and careful men

Lift down a burden thence; and soft within

They set it down in silence; and a moan,

A bitter moan of human agony,

Unheard amid the earlier rush and press,

Arrests the ear, as from the car behind

A group of mourners, wrapped in dusky weeds,

Come forth, and pass beneath our window slow.

To meet them comes another stricken group,

Who waited in the coaches on the left.

Two hoary heads bowed with the weight of grief,

Two strong young men, three women in their prime,

Whose tears flow fast, whose forms like fragile reeds

2*

Bow to the blast of woe.   Those meeting groups

Glide in together, as long-severed streams

That burst their banks and seaward roll as one.

Yet, in their sorrow, one doth claim their care

To whom all turn with tender, deep regard—

A girl-like creature, robed in widow's weeds,

With modest beauty gleaming through her tears.

" Our daughter "—" sister "—" be our hearts thy home ;"

" Thy Henry "—" mine ! " " oh, God ! support us all ! "

She's gently folded to *his* father's breast,

Her young head nestles in *his* mother's arms,

His brothers clasp her to their heart of hearts,

His sisters sweetly kiss her tears away.

" Poor Henry ! " passes round from lip to lip

Till strangers weep to hear.

"All hands aboard ! "

The strong steed gathers up his slackened might,

And forward springs again.   Behind us far

That hearse is moving, with its mournful train

Of aching bosoms to " poor Henry's " home—

His boyhood's happy home.

So goeth life.

Its countless travelers all as one rush on,

Yet each within his bosom holds a world—

A world of joys no other understands,

A world of cares no other shoulders bear,

A world of griefs sealed at their fountain-head,

No other hands can trouble in their depths,

Nor eyes can weep away.

And breaking hearts

And pulseless bosoms mingle with the throng,

Unquestioned and unknown.   The widow mourns

For her lost love alone ; the aged sire

And stricken brothers feel their griefs apart ;

The mother's " Henry " hath her visit lone,

Her sorrowing, last "good-night," ere "dust to dust ! "

She for the living lives and smiles again,

But o'er her dead in stealthy silence weeps.

Forever onward rolls the living tide,

Though drop by drop is lost beside the way ;

Cold Business scarcely falters in his speed

To leave the Silent Passengers at home.

LIFE.

When first the mother clasps her child
    With all a mother's joy—
A hallowed guest, that undefiled
    And velvet-fingered boy;
When first she feels the throbbing heart
    Which on her bosom leans,
And kisses off the tears that start
    As soon as life begins;
Then, could her vision pierce the sheet
    Enfolding all his doom;
Perchance to watch his restless feet
    Throughout a path of gloom;
Could she foresee the thorns and snares
    That wait his hurrying steps,
That toil must come, and anxious cares
    Seal darkly brow and lips;

Could she foresee his heart astrain
   Till quivers all its chords,
While human monsters mock its pain,
   With keen, insulting words;
Would she not kiss her baby's brow
   With wild, beseeching prayer,
That God would take the darling now
   Home to His heavenly care?
Home, ere a drift of passion crossed
   That forehead's placid snow—
Home, ere a wave of anguish tossed
   The bosom lake below?

When first the father sees with pride
   His petted lamb progress
In knowledge, growing at his side
   To statelier loveliness;
With all the ways, so sweet and coy,
   Which render childhood dear,
Ere nature blends with art's alloy
   Our household jewels here;

Had he the power, for once, to tear

   The veil from future years,

And see that hearthstone idol bear

   Its load of grief and fears ;

Before his dearest hopes were crushed,

   His glories turned to dust ;

Ere scorn his notes of gladness hushed,

   Or treachery mocked his trust ;

E'en as he clasped that clinging one

   Yet closer to his breast,

How would he pray the morning's sun

   Might shine on him at rest—

At rest, the things that perish here

   Beneath the friendly sod—

Mute lips—clasped hands—the shroud—the bier—

   The spirit safe with God.

What art thou, Life? A fearful race

   For kings and slaves of kings ;

A weary hand, a fruitless chase

   For moth and shadow-wings ;

The rainbow gilds the hours before, ,

  To fade whene'er we come ;   ʻ

The darkness of the past, in store,

  Looms forward to the tomb ;

No bosom life is e'er revealed,

  Till all its hours are sped.

Oh ! tearful history, wisely sealed

  Till all that dies is dead !

Then, where no earthly discord jars

  Upon the calm sublime,

The angel of the eternal stars

  Unclasps the Book of Time.

" The Roll of Time ! " his voice proclaims—

  The startled worlds bow down ;

The nations answer to their names,

  And every soul his own.

POETS LOVE POETS.

Poets, in your bosoms hiding
  Love no other bosoms feel,
Lone and wearily, abiding
  'Midst the hearts to you of steel;
Looking back o'er time's dark surges,
  Dreaming of the years to come,
Till from fancy's mould emerges
  Wondrous forms of joy or gloom,
And the present sweet, or sorrow,
Only rims the great to-morrow.

Poets by the world derided,
  Crowded, jostled, yet alone,
Link from kindred link divided,
  Wed to souls of other tone—
Souls that pity your endeavor,

Now, to set aflame the spark
Which shall struggle on forever
Through the future's gleam and dark;
Souls that chafe to see ye keeping
Vigils when the world is sleeping.

Poets from the world inditing
" Thoughts that breathe and words that burn,"
Poets, all too meek for writing,
Singing in your heart's deep urn ;
Night-dew on your foreheads glistening,
Reverent treading path and sod ;
Child-like on the green-sward listening
To the under-tones of God ;
Watchers in the dim room sitting,
Deeds your prayers, where life is flitting.

Poets hear ! and answer truly :
Whatsoe'er your names or lots,
Whomsoe'er your friends, that duly
Share your palaces or cots ;

Maids, or men to love that win you—

Mother, sister, brother, wife,

Lives there not one cord within you,

Deep within your inmost life,

Voiceless, tender, sad and lonely,

Whispering "love" to poets only?

I DO NOT LIKE TO HEAR HIM PRAY.

I do not like to hear him pray
　Who loans at twenty-five per cent.,
For then I think the borrower may
　Be pressed to pay for food and rent.
And in that Book we all should heed,
　Which says the lender shall be blest,
As sure as I have eyes to read,
　It does not say " take interest."

I do not like to hear him pray
　On bended knee about an hour,
For grace to spend aright the day,
　Who knows his neighbor has no flour ;
I'd rather see him go to mill
　And buy that luckless brother bread,
And see his children eat their fill,
　And laugh beneath their humble shed.

I do not like to hear him pray

   " Let blessings on the widow be!"

Who never seeks her'home, to say

   " If want o'ertakes you, come to me."

I hate the prayer so loud and long

   That 's uttered for the "orphan's weal,"

By him who sees him crushed by wrong,

   And only with *the lips* doth feel.

I do not like to hear him pray

   With face as long as any rail,

Who never means his debts to pay,

   Because he can't be put in jail;

For caution asks the written bond,

   But friendship trusts the word alone;

And he 's a knave where'er he 's found,

   Who never comes the debt to own.

I do not like to hear her pray,

   With jewelled ears and silken dress,

Whose washerwoman toils all day,

 And then is asked to " work for less."

Such pious " shavers " I despise !

 With folded hands and airs demure

They lift to Heaven their " angel " eyes,

 Then steal the earnings of the poor !

I do not like such soulless prayers ;

 If wrong, I hope to be forgiven ;

No angel's wing them upward bears—

 They 're lost a million miles from Heaven.

I do not like long prayers to hear,

 And studied, from the lips depart ;

Our Father bends a ready ear—

 Let words be few—*He hears the heart.*

WOMAN THE FOE OF WOMAN.

Woman the foe of woman—can it be?
Woman should be all love, all charity;
No dark suspicion through her soul should steal—
She should go forth to comfort and to heal;
To cheer the tempted as they strive to stand,
And if they fall, to give a helping hand;
To scatter flowers in the path of woe,
Is woman's mission to the world below.
Should she fling serpents in a sister's face,
Or her pure lips be linked with her disgrace?

God doth uphold *thee*, who is over all—
He, in His wisdom, lets thy sister fall;
God is the judge of both—let her beware,
And glory not, whose feet escape the snare!

Hast thou not sinned? say, in some evil hour,

Has no wild passion sought thy bosom's bower?

Has no black line that bosom's whiteness crossed?

No waking virtue in a dream been lost?

Hast *thou* not sinned? O, ponder and defer;

When *thou art pure,* first cast a stone at her.

Woman relentless, iron-browed and stern,

Watching her sister's steps at every turn

Of life's sad way, with loud, indignant calls,

Bidding the world to "brand her," as she falls,

Is not true woman, though she bears her name,

For the true woman mourns her sister's shame,

Steals to her chamber when the world's asleep,

Not to upbraid her, but with her to weep;

Kisses the lips by agony made white,

And whispers "Jesus" with her soft good-night.

THE UNSEEN.

A whisper in the inward ear,
  As south winds in the flowers sigh ;
A vision floating in the clear
  Cerulean of the spirit's eye ;
Foretasting of a coming bliss,
Foreshadowing of a bitterness,
  A call when none is nigh.

A strain of music soft and low,
  As morning breaks the web of dreams,
And forms that rested long ago
  Go out, as in the daylight streams ;
It was their breath that swept our hair,
They smiled and beckoned in the air,
  Then hid in morning's beams.

As noon appears, with florid face
  And stifled breath we seek the shade,
To muse in some sequestered place,
  Which love or grief hath sacred made ;
Where murmuring brook and singing bird
Alone the waves of sound have stirred,
  Since verdure clothed the glade.

E'en there, as zephyrs part the leaves,
  And sweep the blossoms with their wings,
We hear a voice ; it chides or grieves,
  It whispers low, it softly sings ;
A shadow trembles on the grass,
We list to hear a footstep pass ;
  What hand that leaflet flings?

And oft as evening shadows steal
  O'er meadows green and hills of brown,
The mystic mingling with the real,
  White fingers part the Day-God's crown,
Familiar faces smile ; between

3

The rosy sunset's pencilled sheen,

    The loved and lost look down.

Yet gazing there with yearning sight,

    A fairy ship attracts the view;

We see her climb the waves of light;

    With gauzy sails and shadowy crew,

Fast onward o'er the darkling deep

She hurries with mysterious sweep,

    And trackless leaves the blue.

Fair wanderer! whither goest thou

    So stilly in the ethereal main?

She makes no sign—she's fading now—

    Her crew have shrunk to specks again.

Far where the shimmering sunset dies

Her sails fade out; our weary eyes

    Seek her dim port in vain.

Oh! voices hushed so long in death,

    And forms beloved we 've missed so long,

Why hear we still in under-breath
   The floating fragments of your song?
Ye live! ye live! it must be so;
Unseen ye come, and whisper low
   Amidst the angel throng.

CREEDS.

What countless creeds are based on One who died,

Though all for pardon seek His bleeding side;

One prayer ascends from every bended knee,

" ' Our Father ' help us, as we trust in Thee."

One Hand we see in every change below,

The winds obey Him and the lightnings know;

The earthquake comes obedient at His call,

The city sinks—centurial columns fall.

The sea upheaves a continent to light,

An Isle is born—another sinks in night;

He "turns and overturns" from pole to pole,

Upholds the stars—yet stoops to save a soul.

As *I* have loved thee, even unto death,

Love thou thy brother, the Redeemer saith;

Defer to him thy interest and thy will,

And though he wound thee, by thou faithful still ;

Rejoice with him—in sorrow be thou there,

Put thy own shoulder 'neath his load of care ;

If hungry, feed him ; is he thirsty? give

From thy own well-spring, bid him drink and live.

Who is thy "brother?" ponder well the word ;

The poorest servant of the common Lord :

Where'er he dwells, whate'er his faith or name,

The bond fraternal holds ye both the same.

Let neither claim the right to lead and rule,

Nor "judge" his brother, nor pronounce him "fool."

"As a man thinketh," say ye, "so is he ;"

As a man *doeth* so his end shall be.

Prove thy *faith better* by thy *better deeds*

Than his thou doubtest, nor contend for "creeds."

Creeds are of earth ; we lose them in the strife

With the last Foeman of our mortal life ;

One "welcome home!" awaits the good and pure

Where prayers and rituals and all tears are o'er.

Jesus! thy jewels, born of every faith,

Bear but *one value* in Thy blood-bought wreath.

A PRAYER.

Help me, O, God! to bring at last to Thee
A soul as pure as human soul may be!

If in the flush and vanity of youth
I turned me lightly from the path of truth;
O'er softer nature pride's cold mantle hung,
And calmly smiled when grief my bosom wrung;
Gave answer lightly to the child of care,
And hurried on scarce noting her despair;
The toiling student met with haughty brow,
Nor said "my brother!"—God forgive me now!
Passed on, nor heard a mother's warning voice,
To festive pleasures wildering glare and noise;
Bent low to catch the whispered words of praise,
Nor heeded Thine who claimed those better days:

Forgive me, Thou who know'st the reckless beat
Of life's young pulse, for hope has proved a cheat !

Amid the scenes and cares of later life,
If I have erred as mother, friend or wife ;
If, worn with toil, I 've met in wayward mood
The bold inquiry of the kind and good ;
If, chained to want, my heart has sighed in vain
For titled honors, and for golden gain ;
If, tired at night, I 've lain my aching head
With prayerless tongue upon the welcome bed,
Forgot the blessings of the day and week,
And slept with tears yet trickling o'er my cheek—
Tears wrung by anguish from the heart that pride
Locked up all day, and loosed at eventide :
Forgive me, God ! thou know'st my weary lot,
And in Thy mercy be my sins forgot !

CRUSHED HOPES.

Life, how thy hopes have fled !
  As morning's broken dreams,
As rolling sands on ocean's bed,
As dust upon the gossamer thread,
   As starlight's cloud-quenched beams ;
    As scattered spray,
As myriad insect's wings
  Which glitter and are gone ;
As shadowy forms which fancy brings,
Of long-lost friends and perished things ;
So, youth, thy hopes have flown
    Away—away !

As moonbeams gild the eaves
  At evening's hallowed hour,
And, silver-fingered, part the leaves
Where, 'mong the vines the spider weaves
  3*

Her web from flower to flower,

Nor linger here;

As, far where vision breaks

Upon the vast—vast sea,

White sails are seen, as tiny specks,

And wondering we if ships or wrecks

Are borne away to lea,

And disappear.

As fragments of a song,

We would recall again,

Whose bird-like notes we've missed so long,

Are lost amidst the countless throng

Of memories on the brain—

Of cares and lore;

As passed that zephyr's breath,

As young life's laughter hushed,

As gathered blossoms in the wreath

On beauty's brow fold up in death;

So have my hopes been crushed,

To rise no more.

PLANTING A TREE.

I am planting a tree—'t is love's labor ; I know
It will never for me to maturity grow ;
It will number its summers, and whiten with 'time,
When I dwell 'mid the blooms of the shadowless clime.

I am planting a shade where a sorrowful one
Will repeat, in hushed accents, " the planter is gone ;"
And my own hearthstone darlings, apart and afar,
Will but sit in its shadow in memory's parterre.

O, never my lips, though my spirit will sigh
In the cool of its branches that climb to the sky ;
But if one human brother shall rest in its shade,
And take heart for life's battle anew, I 'm repaid.

PLANTING A TREE "THE WRONG END UP."

I was planting a row of saplings one day,
And my wits were flighty—they are alway—
I spaded, and settled them here and there,
Like a row of corn, all even and fair;
But I said, as my thoughts on one were bent,
I will make of this an experiment;
Where the buds were born the roots shall grow,
And the buds shall stretch into roots below;
Then I cut off the roots, so newly born,
And planted it deep and straight as corn.

But I waited in vain for the buds to burst
From the tall, thin trunk of the tree reversed;
There it lingered, devoid of verdure and sap,
Till I flung it away, and filled the gap.

Since the day of that planting I 've traveled some,

And have met on life's turnpike more fools than one ;

But I never have met a woman or man

Bewailing the wreck of some foolish plan,

But I 've said in my heart, "You deserved this cup,

For planting your sapling ' the wrong end up.' "

BREAD AND BUTTER.

Cries a child beside the gutter,

" Want a piece of bread and butter ; "

Cries the mother, in the door,

" Child, be still—we have no more."

Says the lady, passing by,

With a proud, disdainful eye,

" Little brute in garments tattered,

How my satin he bespattered ;

Filthy woman ! filthy boy !

How the poor the rich annoy ! "

Child still paddles in the gutter,

Loudly crying " bread and butter ! "

On goes *she*, with queen-like mien,

Dazzling many with her sheen ;

Solemn bells are tolling loud,

Goes she with the "pious" crowd ;

Kneels she in the solemn aisle,

Heaps she high that silver pile,

Listens she, with upturned brow,

To that surpliced preacher now,

Sighing, like an angel grieved,

For the souls that ne'er believed ;

Conscience never thinks to utter—

Even *Faith* needs bread and butter.

Says the seamstress, in despair,

Toiling, with neglected hair,

From the break of morn till night,

Till her blue eyes lose their light,

And her heart doth wildly flutter,

" God ! how dear is bread and butter ! "

Says her mistress, tall and thin,

" God makes some to toil and spin ;

Thank Him for the strength thou hast,

None who work have need to fast ;

Shame on any one to mutter,

Who can earn her bread and butter."

Rings a voice throughout the halls

Where the sunlight never falls—

Through that damp and dismal keep,

Where the wretched curse and weep,

" Want and sorrow brought *me* here,

Wages low, and flour dear ;

Starving children cried for bread,

Famished wife lay low in bed ;

One my hard-earned wages kept,

And I slew him as he slept !

God ! thou know'st the truth I utter,

He withheld my bread and butter."

Says the client, " I 'm in trouble,

Help me, and I 'll fee you double ;

Stating then the case's merit,

What he rightly should inherit,

Lawyer answers, "Ah, of course,

Many a cause than yours is worse;

Justice you must surely get—

Cannot fail—my head I 'll bet;

Leave the whole to me, I say

' Where there 's will there is a way.' "

Exit client—hear him mutter

" Right or wrong, *my bread I 'll butter!* "

Says a lady, weak and pallid,

(Dined on lobster, pig and salad,)

" Doctor, I am growing ill—

Need a powder or a pill."

Doctor takes her wrist and sighs,

" *Very ill*, to my surprise !

Go to bed—I 'll try to cure you,

Life, e'en now, I can 't insure you;

Take to-night these pills eleven,

And to-morrow powders seven."

Home she goes with saddened brow;

" Ha !" says he, " I have her now;

Doubts not she a word I utter,

And I *lie* for bread and butter."

Says the preacher to his flock,

" Hide you in the 'Living Rock,'

Whatsoe'er your work or name,

God doth love you all the same."

And a pattern pastor he

Seemeth in reality.

But when *coarse-wooled* lambkins stray,

Never does he ask "which way?"

Goes not far to bring *them* in,

Leaves them wandering in their sin.

When the "sheep" of golden fleeces

Break the fold, the "shepherd" chases;

Finds the wanderers—brings them back,

(Knows *whose wool must fill his sack*)—

Earnest blessings then doth utter

O'er recovered "bread and butter."

Politicians, to and fro,

Working for " the people," go,

Never minding wind or weather,

Here they whisper, there they gather,

Making friends, and making speeches,

Sucking good men's blood like leeches—

Puff *themselves*, the modest fellows !

Self-inflating, noisy bellows !

Puff " the people," till " the people "

Lift them high as any steeple ;

" Sov'reign people "—" people dear "—

(Generous people, it is clear,)

So " hurrah ! " they take their station,

Sov'reigns of a " sov'reign nation,"

Which they 'll prove to demonstration :

On " the people's " shoulders set—

Ho ! for a ride, with a galling bit—

Ride, and run, and spur, and sputter,

On " the people's " bread and butter.

Dreamed a dream too sad to utter,

Saw a wide, terrific gutter,

Not of water, but of fire—
Smoke up-curling, higher—higher—
There a lady cried for "water,"
Who had scorned the poor man's daughter;
There a lawyer sorrowing, said,
" I consumed my client's bread ; "
And a doctor cried, "I filled her
With my drugs, and robbed and killed her—
Frightened, blistered, leeched and cut her,
All to make my bread and butter."

There the politician moaned,
" While my country bled and groaned,
I, the people's neck astride,
Had a most exalted ride ;
Eating up their bread and butter,
Who had raised me from the gutter ;
' Honorable ' then they thought me,
Me, whose lies a title bought me ;
No man says ' your servant ' here—
' Bought my whistle very dear.'

'T is a 'democratic' gutter,

All are minus bread and butter."

Saw I not that baby there,

With his little brow of care,

Nor his mother, in the door,

Saying, "child, we have no more."

There, was not that man of woe,

Who for bread had slain his foe,

Nor that seamstress, pale and sad,

Who had sold her fame for *bread;*

There, were not those *coarse-wooled* sheep

Whom no shepherd tried to keep—

Not a spirit walked that gutter,

Who had starved for bread and butter.

There the haughty head was low,

Naked was the mitred brow ;

Kings were there, without their crowns,

Priests were there, without their gowns,

Lawyers, doctors, minus fees,

Nabobs, minus beds of ease ;

But the sorrowing ones of earth,

Penury's children from their birth,

Dwellers lone in caves and sheds,

Taunted from their cradle-beds,

God had pitied and forgiven,

Purified, and called to Heaven.

With this dream, so sad to utter,

Ends my song of " bread and butter."

THE SIGN OF THE WIDOW McCREE.

Pray who is that man in the broad-cloth and satin,

With a neckerchief stiff and a slick beaver hat on,

In cassimeres fine as a king ever sat on ;

With two little gray eyes, and a nose with a turn up,

Like a pigtail that 's roasting, and ready to burn up,

Or a little, grey kitten, adrift, with its *stern* up ;

Who seems fretted and worn, as an over-tasked waiter,

Making speed at the rate of a holiday skater?

Who is he?   Do n't you know?

That is Squire Van Blow,

Who is hurrying so,

All in black, like a crow,

From his crown to his toe.

He has millions and billions,

The more is the pity,

Twelve farms in the country,

Ten blocks in the city;

He has horses and cattle, and sheep without number;

He has coal beds, and forests, and mills to saw lumber,

Velvet slippers and gown,

In a palace up town,

Where he snores upon down,

And choice wines bring sweet dreams to his slumber

But the Squire, you see,

Has a sister, McCree,

Who—for such things will be—

Far away was at work, and aggrieving;

She wrote him sometimes,

From his surplus of dimes,

(This he ranked among crimes,)

To send her what he well could be giving;

And he wearied of her—

Her " Dear brother—dear sir,"

And thought none would infer

That his sister Maria was living.

So he wrote her he could n't,

He should n't, he would n't,

Be harassed and troubled :

His business had doubled,

His stores and his stills,

His mines and his mills,

All needed his care and attention ;

Her epistles were many,

Not one worth a penny,

She must not send any,

He desired an immediate suspension.

Then the widow, she said,

With a toss of her head,

He shall wish me quite dead ;

I 'll go back to the place I was born in.

(Who says I shall not?)

There rent me a cot,

With such means as I 've got,

Little better than cribs they put corn in.

4

And Maria McCree,

After settling, you see,

Hung a sign on a tree,

Which her brother descried on the morrow,

" Yellow letters in blue,"

Said she, laughing, " will do,"

As her name rose in view,

" This will give him vexation and sorrow;

I, Maria Van Blow,

All the village will know,

Am now fallen so low

That appearance no longer I borrow;

For promptly attending

To washing and mending,

And taking, and sending

Clothes home, on that shingle, I 've painted,

And nailed to that tree,

(Even so let it be),

By Maria McCree,

With her neighbors aforetime acquainted."

'T is reported he proffered,

From gold he had coffered,

Five hundred; and offered

To send her this way, or another;

But she scorned to be hired—

Said her comfort required

Nothing more; she desired

But to stay within sight of her brother.

Now, we hear he is making

(With agony shaking)

An effort, and taking

All pains to be off to the city;

But the widow declares,

Where he goes, with his heirs,

She will haunt his gray hairs,

And we doubt not she will, for she 's gritty.

All too late, he is wise,

And wherever he hies,

To his shame and surprise,

He will meet the gaunt form of his sister;

City, village, or town,

As he goes up and down,

She will cling to his side like a blister.

There, printer, you 've heard

How he paused and deferred,

By no sympathy stirred,

To be up and a-doing in season;

Till, the golden hours flown,

He transformed into stone

Her sad heart; and his own

Is "in torment" too soon for that reason.

THE WASHING BILL.

Where windows draped in gold and blue'
    Were silvered by the moon,
And massive pillars, wreathed with dew,
    In shadowy splendor shone ;

Where downy cushions offered rest
    To care's o'erlabored head,
And feet on carpet flowers were pressed
    Soft as a mossy bed ;

Where pictures rare, and mirrors vast,
    Were hung in golden frames,
And glittering things, by wealth amassed,
    Flashed like a hundred flames ;

Two ladies sat, discoursing low—
　　High-born and proud they seemed,
As, melting on their forehead's snow,
　　The radiance o'er them streamed.

A fleecy cap the matron wore ;
　　The maiden's auburn hair,
In shimmering ringlets, drifted o'er
　　Her neck and shoulders fair.

The maiden's eye was cold, and set
　　Intensely on her thought ;
Those lips, whose balmy alphabet
　　Was grief's, her curve had caught.

" Say not forgive ; sweet mother, hush !
　　Now comes the avenging hour ;
That craven heart I 've won to crush
　　Shall feel my utmost power."

Lo! enters in a smiling man
 Of fashion and parade,
A bland, obsequious gentleman,
 And bows before the maid.

"Dear Isabel! for e'er the same,
 My worship I repeat;
Our bridal day I pray thee name—
 My life is at thy feet."

The maid replies: "Sit down by me,
 I'll answer by-and-by;
A story let me tell to thee
 Before I make reply:

"Of common life, of common things,
 And hearts that sorrow knew,
A tale where fancy folds her wings,
 And listens to the true."

" Speak on, sweet sov'reign of my will,

    I cannot tell thee nay;

Whate'er thou say'st, my pleasure still

    Is always to obey."

THE TALE.

" A woman, when the wind was raw,

    Wore faded calico;

Her bonnet was the coarsest straw,

    With neither band nor bow.

" Her shoes were neither bound nor lined,

    Her hose of rope-like yarn,

Their first foundation hid behind

    Full many a crafty darn.

" No cloak nor shawl enwrapped her form,

    That cold December day,

When, hurrying through a rising storm,

    She entered on Broadway.

" She stopped before a large hotel,

 Beside a group of men,

And said, to one who knew her well,

 ' Please pay me two pounds ten.'

" I 'm very poor; so small a sum

 Must seem a mite with thee;

I have three tender babes at home,

 Who wait and weep for me.

" Think! I have toiled for many a day

 To make thy linen clean;

Then, come to ask for honest pay,

 Have been denied at e'en.

" Think how I 've come thro' snow and thaw,

 And brought those robes again;

While frightened faces shrieked ' Mamma!'

 At every broken pane.

  4*

" Begone ! he said, I owe thee naught,

Thou bold, untruthful jade,

That well deserv'st a beggar's lot ;

I have no debts unpaid !

" What could she do ?   Derision's laugh

From lip to lip went round ;

Why should she vent her feeble wrath

Where *not a man* was found.

" They do not fear the Holy One,

Who kept her humble fold ;

Whose hand might break their hearts of stone,

Ere half their years were told.

" That night, all night, resolved she stood,

And washed, and rinsed, and wrung ;

Her only hope of flour and wood

On that night's labor hung.

" The angel saw her desperate strife,
  Who stood to guard her door,
And prayed the Author of her life,
  She thence might toil no more.

" A brother dear, in manhood's morn,
  To distant isles had sailed ;
Life's burden and its heat he 'd borne,
  Nor once his kindred hailed.

" With wealth untold that pilgrim came,
  A man of silvered hair,
His earthly goods, his honored name,
  With friends beloved to share.

" For parents dear his bosom yearns :
  They 've passed within the door
Which opes for all, but whence returns
  Not one, forever more.

" His sister's name he seeks, with dread,
    On each memorial stone ;
She sleeps not 'mong his household dead—
    Where has the loved one gone ?

" She *should* be known in many a hall
    Which once she graced with him ;
They knew her once, so far and tall,
    Now long unknown to them.

" They kept her image while it smiled,
    Within a jeweled case ;
They lost it when, misfortune's child,
    She wore a graver face.

" He seeks her here, he seeks her there ;
    None know the changed Jeannette,
Till chance reveals the aged pair
    Who note the sufferer yet.

" My tale is told.   O, shrunken soul !
   Why are thy lips so white ?
  Thy laundress, like a beckoning ghoul,
   Shall scare thy dreams to-night !

" Thy laundress, in that velvet grey,
   All edged with golden sheen,
  Who turns her tearful face away,
   Tho' here at home a queen.

" And I am one of three that wept
   When ' mother ' staid so long,
  And, shivering on the hearth-stone, kept
   The record of her wrong.

" For this one hour the net was spread
   Which holds thy feet so fast ;
  I break its meshes, thread by thread ;
   Go ! I 'm avenged at last.

" Unhappy man ! the bond was loosed,

He lost, but loved her still,

Who, fifteen years before, refused

Her mother's Washing Bill."

BETTER OUT OF THE WORLD THAN THE FASHION.

Queen Fashion, you know, is a wonderful shrew,
If she says "wear pink," lay aside your blue;
Or she'll tell all the world to laugh at you—
   Oh! how ridicule puts the lash on;
Get out of the world, if you're poor and proud,
While your credit is good for a coffin and shroud;
For we'll tell you a secret—don't breathe it aloud —
   "Better out of the world than the fashion."

Speak humbly and low in the rich man's ear;
Though your heart be breaking, suppress that tear;
For he "hates long stories," he says with a sneer,
   And your "labor" you won't get the "cash on."
Hush! say he is generous, and kind, and good,
Though he's greedily sucking your very blood,

And would tear the last rag from your back, if he could,

   For, to flatter the rich *is the fashion.*

Speak softly, O bard! when you sing your song;

Most gently, O preacher! nor preach too long;

Never mention omissions, nor things done wrong,

   Or your people will fly in a passion;

Plain talk was a folly of olden times,

But should never appear in our modern rhymes;

And that preacher may whistle for hearers and dimes

   Whose sermons are *out of fashion.*

Just pleasantly tell them *how pious they are,*

With a bow and a smile, and they'll all be there—

'What an excellent sermon'—'a beautiful prayer'—

   And they'll give you enough to dash on.

Do likewise, O poet! the time has gone by

When your pathos was answered by tears in the eye,

And *the truth,* as a poem, is bitter and dry,

   And wofully *out of fashion.*

TWIN SPIRITS.

We tell you never was a soul created,
  But that another was created for it ;
Though here and there antipodes are mated,
  There are "*twin spirits*," and we underscore it ;
It sometimes happens blundering chance has led them
So far asunder earth can never wed them,
  And so for Heaven they wait.

We tell you, too, if two have been united,
  Of different tastes and adverse education,
By any freak of fortune, or short-sighted
  Advice of friends, without consideration,
They find their "union" but a bursting bubble,
Never in anything but folly double,
  Till they agree *to hate.*

Look to it! ye who yet unfettered wander,

    Lest mirage waters lure ye to your doom;

Ye will love once—it must be; therefore ponder

    Till life's spring passes, and its summer bloom;

Yea, wait till Autumn's hoary frosts shall find you,

For your "*twin spirit;*" let no other bind you,

    Lest you be wise too late.

SPIES ! SPIES ! ! SPIES ! ! !

Spies upon our hearths intruding,
   Angels shield us from your wiles !
Heaven help us bear in patience
   All the sunshine of your smiles !

Spies that come with curls and kisses,
   Sighing o'er our griefs and cares ;
Never mind *our* trouble, darlings,
   Leave *us out* of all your " prayers."

Spies that stand at every corner,
   Spying "for your country's weal,"
Spying " for religion's honor,"
   Stabbing whom ye feign to heal.

Spies that eat the good man's dinner,

    Taking notes of every word ;

On *his* viands, half digested,

    To repeat the story heard.

Spies that, *in the wool* of "patrons,"

    Seek, like wolves, the trustful young ;

Hungry for the bosom secrets

    Dropping from the thoughtless tongue.

Spies of every grade and station,

    Wise and simple, great and small,

Village, city, army, nation,

    Now are struggling in your thrall.

To your holes, ye parlor vipers !

    To your nests, ye pious owls !

Get ye *home*, infernal pickets !

    Satan calls *his* "muster rolls."

THE WORLD.

The world is an ass, which is goaded along
  By many a bawling fellow;
And she seldom kicks when a fool jumps on,
  Though he spurs till her flanks are mellow.

The world is a child, allured by toys,
  And charmed with bells and rattles;
And the hero who makes the greatest noise,
  Is the hero of all her battles.

The world's a coquette, who spreads her snares
  For the idle and the simple;
And dallies alike with the man of cares,
  Or the boy with the baby-dimple.

The world is a weaver, laughing aloud
   In the midst of the sick and dying,
And cheerily singing while weaving a shroud,
   Or at wedding robes carelessly plying.

The world 's a physician, the pulse that feels
   Of the patient that pays her kindly ;
But the brain of the poor man throbs and reels,
   And " the doctor " goes past him blindly.

The world is a lawyer, pleading the cause
   Of the rich with due precision ;
But the claims of the poor are dark with flaws,
   And she passes them by with derision.

The world is a preacher, reproving sin
   Where the prospect is poor for a dinner ;
But graciously smiling, and crying "clean,"
   Where there 's hope of a feast with the sinner

The world is a critic, deaf, dumb and blind
  To the claims of unlucky merit ;
But, fee her beforehand, she 'll give you "a mind,"
  Though your head be as blank as a garret.

The world is Queen Fashion; her fettered slaves
  She rules with a rod unfeeling ;
And they find no rest till in quiet graves
  They forget her unkindly dealing.

The world—she is everything under the sun !
  It surpasses our art to describe her ;
She will rank us all "idiots," let her alone,
  She will call us all "wise" if we bribe her.

NOBODY.

If nobody 's noticed you, you must be small;

If nobody 's slighted you, you must be tall;

If nobody 's bowed to you, you must be low;

If nobody 's kissed you, you 're ugly, we know;

If nobody 's envied you, you 're a poor elf;

If nobody 's flattered you, flatter yourself;

If nobody 's cheated you, you are a knave;

If nobody 's hated you, you are a slave;

If nobody 's called you a " fool " to your face,

Somebody 's wished for your back in its place;

If nobody 's called you a " tyrant " or " scold,"

Somebody thinks you of spiritless mould;

If nobody knows of your faults but " a friend,

Nobody 'll miss of them at the world's end;

If nobody clings to your purse like a fawn,

Nobody 'll run like a hound when it 's gone;

If nobody's eaten his bread from your store,

Nobody'll call you "a miserly bore;"

If nobody's slandered you—here is our pen—

Sign yourself NOBODY, quick as you can.

5

"UPS AND DOWNS."

Men talk of their "ups" and their "downs,"
    And a wonderful racket they make;
And women in boroughs and towns
    To talk of them oft lie awake.

I have only to mention of mine,
    That some have had fewer, some more;
And the medium's the thing, I opine,
    So I'll keep discontent out of door.

I have had but a precious few "ups,"
    While my "downs" count a million or so;
But one who on charity sups
    Might envy my station e'en now.

These words can be strangers to none,

    Yet few on their import agree ;

For what is the " up " of the one,

    The "down " of another might be.

THE THIRST FOR FAME.

A hoary mortal whom the world called "great,"
Unsated still with praise, defying God,
Stole from the crowd to battle with himself,
And voiced his heart-throes thus in bitter words :

Fame, how I wooed thee !   With my strong, wild will
I trampled down the flowers.   I spurned the grass ;
I would not note the innocent child at play,
Nor hear life's mentor, bowed with hoary age ;
I talked not with the stars—the pensive stars—
That hung above me, high and pure alway !
I hailed no God's hand in the concave blue,
Nor knelt before him in the midnight's hush.
But when the cloud rolled up its inky folds,
And the forked lightning cut its way amain ;

When the hoarse tempest rocked the startled earth

Till the roused ocean battled with the shore,

And shrieking sea-birds flecked the plain with white ;

Then my lips smiled, as answered bolt to bolt,

And fiercer lightnings lit the shuddering dark ;

For all my being was for fame athirst.

One hot, mad fever fired my heart and brain;

And hours were years, and years as lustrums were

Till the world knew me ; but I thirsted still.

Alas ! ambition, in thy direful wake

Lie throngs of broken hearts—cold, ghastly piles

Of hearts, that perished in the covered fires

Thy torch had kindled and thy breath had fanned !

Must I walk softly to those myriad heaps

While yet my name is but a whispered word?

God of this weary soul ! if madest thou me

To crawl life's highway like a slimy worm,

Why didst thou make my heart a living coal,

To rock and kindle in the strong, wild wind?

Is here no rest, but for those plodding feet

That never spurn the dust?   Then welcome, toil !

And let me nurse these bosom-embers still,

And with my last breath fan their crimson back.

HOW TO PLEASE EVERYBODY.

Rise in the morning as early as five,

And work for the drones that lie snug in the hive ;

Breakfast on water, for coffee is dear,

Save for the visitors all your good cheer ;

Shut the door softly, and rush to your work,

But if any man hail you, hold up, with a jerk ;

His questions all answered, then hurry along,

Giving all of the path to each child of the throng ;

Stop, though you 've not leisure, to chat with the fool,

And talk with the minions of cant and misrule ;

Bow to the great man, and shrink from the rich,

Till your feet in their humbleness plunge in the ditch.

Arrive at your work shop precisely at 'leven,

Though you meant to have reached it an hour before seven ;

Toil like a dog till the clock has struck one,

Then turn your face homeward, your task scarce begun ;

And, if all your friends happen at dinner to be,

You may get to your lodgings sometime before three.

Send your boy to the priest with your mutton and wine,

And on brown bread and water contentedly dine;

Tell your wife, if she asks for a dollar, to "wait,"

And give two to the beggar that stands at your gate;

Give your *last* to the lady who asks you for some

"For the perishing heathen," though robbing your home;

If your pocket cry "emptiness," stifle its breath,

For the world must be pleased, though want choke you to
　　　　death.

Then go back to your work, not forgetting to be

"Your obliged," and "your servant," to all whom you see.

Ply your tools like a Hercules now for your bread,

Nor go home till you're certain the world is in bed;

Take a crust for your supper, lie down upon hay,

And dream over the friendships made fast through the day.

And as this day has passed, let your days all pass on,

Till you've pleased all the world, and your duty is done.

Then lie down and rejoice at the end of your race,

You may own as much land as will cover your face.

Then the "saints" of the world, when they hear of your

    death,

Will exclaim, "Oh, poor fellow!" and draw a long breath,

And pass on unconcerned. 'Ho! you slumbering elf,

If you'd "please everybody" now—*bury yourself.*

5*

GENTLEMAN BEFORE MARRIAGE.

My dearest duck; my sweetest girl,
  I love you most sincerely;
I 'd rather own this sunny curl
  Than win a fortune yearly;
This little hand, so soft and white,
  Was only made for kisses;
This little form, so frail and light,
  Was made for gauzy dresses!

I 'll keep my Kate a span of greys,
  A carriage and a pony;
I 'll go with her to balls and plays,
  And never speak of money;
For her I 'll buy romances new—
  Attending to her pleasure—

And poems, bound in gold and blue,
    I 'll order for my treasure.
Our lives shall be but one sweet dream
    Of love and sunny weather,
No adverse wave shall cross the stream
    Of wedded bliss forever !

AFTER MARRIAGE.

You always talk of plays and balls ;
    You are forever flirting,
And scribbling rhymes, and making calls,
    And never making shirting ;
You smile in every whiskered face ;
    You chase all silly fashions ;
You load with jewels, flaunt in lace,
    And show your angry passions !

The baby 's left to cry and moan,
    I 've ne'er a decent dinner ;

You drag me out, you call me down—
    I am a hen-pecked sinner,
An abject slave—I tell you so!
    Madame! your folly's ended;
You shall not flirt—and go—and go—
    I'm weary and offended;
I'm going to a reading room—
    I'll join a club thereafter—
So—mend your manners—stay at home,
    And dry your eyes with laughter!

LADY BEFORE MARRIAGE.

I feel a very solemn sense
    Of all a woman's duty
To keep within the door-yard fence,
    Unmindful of her beauty;
To share her husband's griefs and cares,
    And, in his shadow walking,
Content to mind her own affairs,
    Be reverent when he's talking!

'T is plain, our Maker did design

    That woman should be humble ;

Not given to looks, nor dressing fine,

    Which makes them fret and grumble.

Those novels are pernicious things

    To feed imagination ;

All filled with angels shorn of wings—

    To me they are vexation.

Dear William, as your wedded wife,

    I never mean to teaze you ;

My aim and pride through all my life

    Shall only be to please you !

AFTER MARRIAGE.

Bill ! come down stairs ; I know you can !

    The baby has the colic ;

The way you shirk your duties, man,

    Is truly diabolic !

The nurse has such a blundering way

    She cannot stop its crying,

And as for me, I'm housed all day
Till I am almost dying!

Ann! run and bring my velvet sacque,
My parasol and bonnet;
I'm going to the Messrs. Black,
The printers, with a sonnet!
I have no time to write nor read
But while *he* tends the baby;
You, Sarah, take this book with speed
Across to Mrs. Maybe;
Ask her to loan me Hugo's last
In change for Love's Dilemma;
There Bill—don't rock so horrid fast—
You'll wake my darling Emma!

"O! IT IS HARD, LINK AFTER LINK."

O ! it is hard, link after link
  To lose from love's bright chain,
And trembling on the grave's cold brink
  Where life's sweet clay is lain,
Repeat the words, " Thy will be done ! "
The heart with such a dismal moan,
  Says, " Can they rise again ? "

Forgive, O God ! the yearning beat
  Of these poor hearts of clay,
That leave with slow, reluctant feet,
  The earth-clods where they lay ;
The faith that still, with leaden wings,
Looks upward to eternal things,
  And cannot soar away.

Could but a voice—a single tone—
   Come from that far-off strand
Where death hath gathered, one by one,
   The cherished household band ;
Could but one tress we 've known before
Float back from that mysterious shore,
   That cloud-wrapped *better land;*

We could believe—we would be still,
   And say, " What is, is right " ;
Yea, with a stern triumphant will,
   Bid all our fears good night.
Grant us a " sign," O risen Lord,
The faintest touch, the lightest word,
   One little beam of light.

WHEN WILL THE MORNING BE?

Father! the night is long and drear;
　　Where doth the morning stay?
When will the first grey tint appear
　　Which ushers in the day?　　　.

When will the first bright silver thread
　　Be woven with the black,
And gladness through the heart be shed,
　　So long on sorrow's rack?

I bear, I strive, nor yield to tears;
　　I hope, believe and trust;
But oh! these long, these weary years!
　　Lord, what am I but dust?

I 'm sick with hope deferr'd—I die ;

Remove this cup from me !

Hushed midnight wearies of my cry—

When will the morning be ?

NAY, NEVER SAY, "POOR!"

Nay, never say, " poor ! "
Lest your friends bring you garments so threadbare and
greasy
You will turn from the sight of them sick and uneasy,
While you dolefully thank them, and think, as you bear it,
That to-morrow you 'll hang the same high in the garret;
To cobwebs you 'll doom them ;
The moth shall consume them
Till light shall illume them ;
The mouse and her young in the pockets shall hide ;
Long life to the donor
Who makes you the owner
Of hapless old trowsers, too short and too wide.

Nay, never say, " poor ! "
And then put up your lip to be kissed so sincerely ;

They will just make a bow, or shake hands with you merely,

Who a short time ago were " so happy to meet you,"

That you feared, in their earnest devotion, they 'd eat you ;

    Now their " How do you do ? "

    Will be solemn and low

    As the plaint of a crow,

When the corn is all gone and the winter is near ;

    They will murmur of " losses,"

    " Disappointments " and " crosses,"

With their eyes on the door ; and, in haste, disappear.

    Nay, never say, " poor ! "

All the world, like your friends, will at once under-rate you ;

Your relations, offended, will shun you and hate you ;

All the fools whom you meet will make bold to advise you

To go this way, or that ; since they 've learned to despise

    you ;

    They will tauntingly say,

    With their drawling " Good-day ! "

    " He who gave takes away,

And the blessings He grants us are oft-times a snare ;"

Then leave you to gather

Your hay in cold weather,

When the fall rains have come and the meadows are bare.

Nay, never say, "poor!"

All the faults of your youth will be whispered and told;

All the secrets, once hidden by glitter and gold;

All the *nothings* you've said in your hurry or spleen,

Will be held up to view without mercy or screen.

Nay, never say, "poor!"

Keep a coach as before;

Borrow money the more;

And, when no man will trust you, take poison and die;

Then your kindred will kiss you,

As they tell "how they'll miss you;"

You will have a fine funeral, and—*creditors cry.*

"ROOT ON!"

Ye men, with faces long and sad!

Ye women, who forever gad

To ferret out the faults, so bad,

    Of all the people near you!

Ye owls in pants!—ye skirted geese!

Who never give our ears release,

Nor grant our souls a moment's peace,

    We will not stoop to hear you.

Oh! fools! with everlasting tongues—

With iron heels and leathery lungs;

Ye barrels, full, with leaky bungs,

    We neither love nor fear you!

There 's not a name on earth so fair

Ye would not set your blotting there,

And finger it with *pious* care

    Till naught remains but sorrow;

There 's not a heart whose generous beat

Ye do not try to prove a cheat ;

Its virtues hide—its faults repeat,

    Where'er ye bid " Good-morrow ! "

The swine, which delves for meaner things,

The jewel to the sunlight flings !

Root on ; till safe where angels' wings

    Ye cannot beg nor borrow !

NATURE.

Like a freed prisoner, boldly walk I forth
Communing with my thoughts.   The earth is mine,
With all its verdure and its glittering dews,
Its waters and its hills.   The low, meek flowers,
Up-springing at my feet, for me exhale
Their wealth of incense ; and I love them all.
I thank thee, Nature ! for thy mountains lift
Their leafy branches proudly o'er my head
To screen me from the sun ; thy rivers flow
On, in their murmuring melody, for aye ;
And the winged warblers of the balmy air
Chant their sweet lays for me.   The evening flings
Her dusky mantle o'er the arching skies,
As weary day retires ; and the fair stars,
As fire-drops glittering on the eternal blue,
Uplift my heart to Heaven.   O Nature ! thou

Good gift of God ! how rich is man in thee !

Thou hast no coffers, but the poorest serf

That treads unlettered on thy common walks

In thee hath heritage.   No robber power

Can wrest from man—the heir—his boundless wealth.

Thou knowest no titles, Nature !   Every child

Of the great Father reigns on earth a prince,

Whose foot-stool is the velvet-coated sward—

Whose throne the hills—whose crown the arch of Heaven !

6

FAREWELL!

Farewell! I press an aching brow;
   Oh! do we look our last?
I cannot love you less, though now
   I blend you with the past;
Farewell! unclasp my throbbing hand,
And grasp it in the "better land!"

THE CARELESS WORD.

I 'll tell you something, neighbors all,
    You need not mind revealing ;
A word is like the graceless ball
    The tumble-bug is wheeling ;
A little piece of dirt, you know,
    When first its owner takes it,
But watch it, and you 'll see it grow
As through the streets she rakes it.

You 'd better never say a word
    Than certain things to mention
Which may be true, but, if they 're stirred,
    Ne'er suffer a declension;
They travel on, from mouth to mouth,
    And magnify in going;
They never stop for rain nor drouth,
    Nor tarry when it 's snowing.

Just like the ball the tumble-bug
    Is rolling, rolling, rolling,
The word which malice gives the tug
    Increases with its bowling;
You utter but a careless thing,
    And hardly know you 've said it,
Till startled by its thundering ring
    Where "bosom friends" have spread it.

LIFE'S UNDER CURRENT.

There is an under current, coursing
   'Neath the surface wave of life,
And the outer and the inner
   Often meet in secret strife ;
But the inner is the stronger,
Darker, deeper, rougher, longer,
   And with dangers rife. .

Look, O man, upon thy brother,
   Ever wavering, nor condemn—
Canst thou know the secret anguish
   Struggling in his bosom, when
He is fitful and unsteady,
Always hurrying—never ready—
   Here, and there again.

Life is full of cares and sorrows
   To each child of Adam's race ;

Care may leave the brow no furrows,
  Smothered passions leave no trace:
Grief may leave no outward semblance
Of the agonized remembrance
  Only one can trace.

Disappointment's canker eateth
  Deep into the bosom's core,
And the proud and tireless watcher
  Guardeth well that bosom's door,
Lest perchance a stranger's finger
Lift the latch where sorrows linger,
  Time ne'er covered o'er.

Chide not then a wayward brother,
  But with all his weakness bear;
Touch his heart-strings lightly, gently,
  Lest a world of grief be there;
And that deep and hidden river
Sweepeth o'er his hopes forever,
  Though a smile he wear.

On its bosom, dark and briny,

   Floateth many a spectral thing ;

And the lost and long lamented

   O'er its waves their shadows fling ;

And the loved and absent meet us—

Walking on its waves they greet us,

   Beckoning—vanishing.

Slighted friendship there reposes,

   Subject to a stubborn will ;

Wounded love his eyelids closes

   While his heart is beating still ;

Passion's fires cast their ashes

On that turbid stream that dashes

   Memory's fount to fill.

Oh ! that dark and dismal river,

   Flowing to the sea of death !

Sweeping in its course forever

   Hope's dead flowers, and Faith's dead wreath.

Under-current darkly flowing,

While life's outer wave is glowing

   Stilly as a breath.

GOD OVER ALL.

Why breaks the heart, because the hand
    Is held so long in thrall,
While slander flings her blazing brand
    To scorch us in our fall?
On God's eternal promise stand,
    For he is over all.

Though friendship fails, and love grows cold,
    And honor turns to dust;
Though human wolves invade the fold
    Of home wherein we trust,
He yet is true who was of old
    The refuge of the just.

Helpless our life-bark seems to go
    On sorrow's stormy sea;
But One is with us who doth know
    Where all the breakers be;
The unseen Pilot whispers low,
    " Be calm, and trust in Me."

SUNSHINE FRIENDS.

As the moth the sunshine flecking
  Are the friends in fortune's train;
From your path the shadow blots them,
  Never to return again.

Sometimes to us in the darkness
  Comes a full hand with a kiss;
For some angel spirits linger
  In a world as cold as this.

But it is not all who meet them—
  They are " far between " and " few ; "
Wait not for their blessed coming—
  They may never come to you.

Weep not for the friends unfaithful;
  Hope not for the friends to come;
Council with the soul within you;
  Up! and work your passage *home!*
    6*

THE SECRET.

I have not told—I will not tell—
 It is my secret yet;
An ice-bound stream—a covered well
 No lips but mine have met.

I thank Thee, God! for power to hide
 Beneath the smile I wear,
The weight of grief—the wound of pride—
 The withered track of care.

I thank Thee none hath power to show,
 Against this stubborn will,
One wavelet of the sea below
 That rolls so dark and still.

In vain inquiring eyes may rest
 On marble brow and cheek;
They cannot pierce the guarded breast,
 And find the thing they seek!

Fight on, O Heart! disguised alone

  In life's mysterious war;

Yet listening to the undertone

  Of promise from afar.

With firmer lip and steadier eye

  Direct thy pilgrim feet;

Nor on thy future's white-leaved sky

  One canceled star repeat.

EARLY MARRIAGES.

You, twenty, saying, " Life is brief,
   And hence I wed to-morrow,"
With ne'er a dollar in relief
   For days of pain and sorrow,
Will find that life is long enough
   When store bills come like hail—
When creditors are growing rough,
   And no man "goes " your " bail."

And, you sixteen, with lily hands,
   In trailing gauze and satin,
That dream of Hymen's silken bands
   O'er books of French and Latin ;
Who make your heaven of dress and forms,
   And all that 's gay and funny ;
Know life's wide sea is flecked with storms—
   Keep close to father's money.

"IT IS NOTHING TO DIE IF YOU'RE NOTED."

It is nothing to die if you're noted,
    And are sure of your guerdon of praise ;
If you're properly married and voted,
    And rode out with your "sorrels" or "greys ;"
If you've had the good sense to keep shady
    While the party nags stood in the stall,
And then sprung to the back of the foremost
    Just in time for "an office next fall."

It is nothing at all to be shrouded,
    If the flags hang half-mast in the bay ;
If you've given the churches ten thousand,
    While you hid half a million away ;
If you've sent a gold cup to a nabob,
    Though you winked at your brother's of tin ;
If your name is in Charity's ledger,
    It is not in man's record of sin.

It is nothing at all to be lying

   With the grave pebbles over your breast ;

If you 've sermonized well at your dying,

   You are " sainted " as well as the best ;

You can list from the ghost-hills delighted,

   While your eulogists thunder and roar,

And read newspaper poems, and stories

   Of yourself never heard of before.

It is nothing at all to be numbered

   With the mortals whose spirits have flown,

If the sins that mortality cumbered

   Through life's glitter and glare were unknown ;

You have leased you an earthly remembrance

   (Though you 've lost upon Heaven your claim)

By your right hand's most royal disbursements,

   Though your left starved your sister to shame.

"FOUND DEAD!"

Chaunt a requiem for our brother!
  Let its notes be soft and low
As the lullaby his mother
  Murmured o'er him long ago ;
For her sweet sake, if she liveth—
For his wife's sake, if one grieveth,
  Be our utterance sad and slow.

Hath he children ? none assembling
  Round him for the last farewell ?
Let our harp strings, faint and trembling,
  For their anguish gently swell ;
For the sakes of all that love him,
Breathe a requiem above him
  Soothing as a holy spell.

For the friends that gathered round him
  When his young pulse gladly beat,

Ere the chains of care had bound him—

    Ere his best hope proved a cheat ;

Sing a song so sad and lonely,

They who hear him then can only,

    When they hear, in sobs repeat.

Peace to thee, O Pilgrim, weary !

    Fallen on life's battle plain ;

Haply, when its hills were cheery,

    Sad misfortune shared thy gain ;

Haply, in its twilight groping

Down the last league, rough and sloping,

    No man asked thy " mite " in vain.

God ! who formed the heart so tender,

    " Frailty " wrote on every string ;

Christ ! thy Saviour and Defender,

    Is thy only judge and king ;

Rest in peace, O stranger brother !

Child afar, or wife, or mother,

    For thy sake this song we sing.

"SERPENTS IN THE GRASS."

Let lions meet me in the way,
 And thunder as they pass ;
But save me, wheresoe'er I stray,
 From "serpents in the grass."

I like the man that 's bold and fair,
 And says, " Behold your foe !
Come meet me openly, and there
 We 'll battle blow for blow ! "

But words are all too weak to tell
 My loathing, my disgust,
For such as feign to love me well,
 And then betray my trust.

HEART LIFE IN CALIFORNIA.

My native land ! my native land !
    A long farewell to thee !
Where setting sunbeams kiss the strand .
    I dwell beside the sea.

Some joys are mine—some jewels flash
    Across my path of pride ;
But oft I turn away to dash
    Regret's hot tear aside.

I love those purpling hills afar,
    Where first I saw the light ;
And cradled 'neath the morning star,
    Slept sweetly in its white.

The heart—the heart too fondly clings
    Unto its earlier home ;

And round its hallowed altar flings
    A glory all its own.

The stranger speaks ; his words are kind ;
    He gives the welcome hand ;
But O ! the tears these eyes that blind—
    How can he understand ?

I cannot share the stranger's load ;
    He cannot help with mine ;
Each treads alone his dreary road,
    And sighs for "auld lang syne."

Familiar forms in visions come
    To meet my earnest gaze ;
I listen for the tones of home,
    As in departed days.

I hide from all one dismal woe—
    One pictured form of clay ;
Whose white lips utter, sad and low,
    Their anguish at my stay.

It were too much ; I could not tear

From out this aching breast

A single memory treasured there,

Till memory's self shall rest.

Accursed gold ! vile yellow dust !

Worms, crawling in thy wake !

Our hearts consume with cankering rust,

And ere we grasp thee—break !

CONFIDANTS!

If you've told a whiskered sinner
    Everything you know,
Go invite him home to dinner
    Every day or so;
Follow him to clubs and races;
    Hug him in the street;
Jostle him throughout life's phases,
    Whispering, "don't repeat!"
Better thus your feet should patter
    Double in and out,
Than your richest " pearls " he scatter
    In some " swinish " route;
If you've had a fair " confessor,"
    Take advice, O fool!
Neither slight her nor oppress her—
    Pet her, and keep cool;

Keep in sight, thou babbling human,
   All that hold thy trust !
Secrets, left with man or woman,
   Seldom stay to rust.

NOBODY WANTS YOU LONG.

As I 've sped on life's errands I 've noticed one thing
   Which, without any charge I 'll impart;
It is this : that the time 'twixt the visitor's ring
   At the door, and " good-bye," should be short;
In the human hive, swarming from morning till night—
Though I 'm sure such a truth I reluctantly write :
      Nobody wants you long.

Hang your hat on that peg but a moment at best,
   And remark, you do n't purpose to stay,
Lest my lady, expecting a welcome guest,
   May be anxious to bid you " good-day ! "
Get you gone, ere her little feet pat on the floor !
And she says in her heart, " What a pitiful bore—"
      Nobody wants you long.

Though your sweetheart consent to be married next fall—

    And we give her much credit for tact—

She's afraid you may meet Lover Two in the hall,

    And a duel might come of the fact;

Then she wants, while yet free, to be gay as a kitten;

Do n't be always on hand, or she 'll give you the mitten."

       Nobody wants you long.

I am naughty, at last, such a secret to mention,

    Which I learned of those men by mere chance;

They begrudge you their time, while they grant you atten-

      tion,

    If you linger all day in their haunts;

Keep your foot on the door-sill, your eye on the clock,

Till you 're off to the counter, the desk, or the dock—

       Nobody wants you long.

A PRAYER FOR PEACE.

Peace, God of Concord! wreathe our blood-stained soil
  With olive blossoms, starting from its red;
Peace, God of Mercy! pour thy healing oil
  O'er wounded bosoms bleeding for their dead;
Peace—Lo! our martyrs ask it at thy throne,
Where earthly passions are no longer known.

Peace! Hear not thou the angry prayer of Hate
  That, wrapped in sackcloth pants and thirsts for blood,
Erect and haughty knocking at thy gate,
  Crying, "Is due me at thy hands, O God!—
My brother's life-lease—and I cannot rest
Until I tear it o'er his prostrate breast."

7

MODERN CHARITY.

Our charity of modern times
   Is seldom found at home ;
She's always "very scant" of dimes,
   When starving neighbors come ;
But builds her churches broad and high,
   And enters there demure ;
Hush ! don't disturb her with your cry—
   She's praying for " the poor."

THE CRITIC.

Write on! the critic scents no common food ;
Shrewd epicurean, what he bites is good ;
He hails the tenderest of the author class,
And says : " Aha !—too poor to buy a pass ! "
Then nails them, shrinking, to his fiendish rack,
While low-mouthed envy titters at his back ;
He mocks the fearful who attempt to sing ;
His barb he buries in the timid wing ;
Write on! ye suffer, but ye shall not die ;
God drops no star from mind's imperial sky ;
Like trampled Truth ye 'll rise with quickened powers,
Whose hardier stalks shall bear immortal flowers.

THE PRAYER OF WASHINGTON.

While the American army lay encamped in a deplorable state of nakedness and starvation at Valley Forge, a Quaker named Potts, passing a secluded spot, heard the voice of some one in prayer. "Stealing quietly forward, he saw Washington's horse tied to a sapling, and a little farther on, in a thicket, was the Chief on his knees, tears streaming down his cheeks, beseeching Heaven for the army and his country."

Where rock on rock is piled,

Where lordly oaks are clasped by graceful vines,

And murmuring brooklets wander through the pines,

And all is rude and wild;

Where leaps from tree to tree

The graceful squirrel—where the wild bird sings

Farewell to autumn, on departing wings,

And hums the busy bee;

There, where no voice is heard,

Save the low insects, mid the brown and green,

And those sweet bird-notes; while the leafy screen

By their light wings is stirred;

There, low on bended knee,
His broad brow lifted to the arching sky,
With folded hands, and meek imploring eye,
He prays, O God! to Thee.

"Father!" His heart is sad
For those poor sufferers yonder in the camp;
Disease is there; their huts are cold and damp;
They ask in vain for bread.

"Father!" In years agone,
A Christian mother taught those lips to pray,
And yet he hears, though youth has passed away,
That gentle teacher's tone.

"Father!" What can he do?
Those hearts, unflinching mid the battle's storm,
Shrink back appalled at famine's haggard form;
How can THE STARVED be true?

Long shadows drape the hill;
His voice alone goes trembling o'er the hush

Which slowly settles over plain and bush,
 Till day's glad pulse is still.

How can he let Thee go !
As Jacob wrestled with his Lord of old,
With breaking heart, yet faith's unbroken hold,
 He wrestles with Thee now.

The precious blessing came—
Long-suffering freedom struggled into birth—
Linked with his country's glory, o 'er the earth
 Echoes his honored name.

"Pray always," One hath said :
Columbia's heart entombs her Washington ;
But who shall say her freedom was not won,
 Because in faith he prayed ?

HOW CAN I FORGIVE?

How can I forgive? they have clouded my brow;
   With the net-work of care they have traced it-;
From my lip and my cheek they have banished the glow,
   Ere the finger of time had effaced it.

How can I forgive! they are crying "aha!"
   As the hopes of my life are receding;
With a laugh and a sneer they are turning away,
   Crushing over the heart that lies bleeding.

How can I forgive? from the depths of despair
   I have cried unto them unregarded;
Yea, they troubled the waves overwhelming me there,
   And my struggle for life was retarded.

How can I forgive? upon Calvary's tree
   Hung a sufferer, blameless forever,
Saying, "Father forgive!" shall a sinner like me
Say, "I will not forgive them?" no—never!

THE POET'S LOT.

The poet's lot
Is an empty cot,
　Whose roof is the upper blue ;
And he measures his song,
Through the nights so long,
　By the rain as it patters through.

The poet's head
On an earthy bed,
　And a wooden pillow lies ;
While the wind doth blow,
And the sheets of snow,
　Come and cover him up to his eyes.

The poet's dreams
Are beautiful beams
　From the land where all is bright ;

And at break of day,

With no debts to pay,

   He sings on with a bosom light.

The poet's rest

Is within his breast,

   Where the cold world can't intrude;

And he eats his crust,

With a humble trust

   In the only Great and Good.

   7*

LIFE'S WORK IS NEVER DONE.

Strange languor through my being stole,
    Unsteady pulses heaved my breast ;
On either cheek a crimson coal,
    Like fire on snow at eve, was pressed ;
Could death be near?   Oh ! not so soon—
My life-star lingered at its noon,
    Far, far away from West.

They told me of those meteor balls
    Which midway from the blue are tossed ;
They bade me mark the leaf that falls
    Ere Summer's drought or Winter's frost ;
" To us " they said " those stars are dim—
That leaf is dead—but not to Him
    Whose works are never lost."

My feet, reluctant, trod the strand
    Where lay beneath the silent sea ;

Beyond it loomed the Better Land,

    Where pain and care no more should be ;

But, backward still my vision turned—

For things behind my spirit yearned,

    And work undone by me.

And there, beside that sea of graves,

    For many months and years I stood

Where Azrael's flag forever waves—

    Oh ! dark, mysterious, sullen flood,

" Go down," they said, " nor wish to stay ;

Their pilot cannot miss the way

    Who put their trust in God."

Alas ! the hopes which death must still ;

    The plans in flower which tears had wet ;

The crushing of that iron will

    Which linked these plans to glory yet ;

High aims, through toil and anguish sought,

Deferred by scorn, to heaven had brought

    The earth-sigh of regret.

Near and more near the billows swept;
  My feet sank in the sliding sands;
Around my brow the coldness crept,
  And touched with ice my ashen hands;
Yet still I prayed, with pulses low,
And white lips stiffening in their woe,
  For life's poor straining bands.

Life! life!" I gasped—my feeble arm
  Yet pleading as my utterance died;
Life's angel caught my sinking form,
  And bore me back from death's dark tide;
He touched my lips with fire anew,
The sluggish current bounded through
  The veins, so shrunk and dried.

But, in my ear he murmured soft,
  "Now speed thy work in faith begun,
For, as I bear thy form aloft,
  Truth's angel whispers 'Never done!
She lives again, to weep—to weave
Bright webs of glass, which straws shall cleave,
  As mesh on mesh is spun.'"

THE PASSING YEAR.

Passing year, thy shadows lay
Heavy on my heart alway;
Backward with regretful look,
Turn I to thy closing book;
Cherished hopes as dreams have sped,
Lights I chased but danced and fled,
And the loved ones, true and tried,
As I leaned upon them, died.
Here I hold a tress of hair;
Yonder stands the "vacant chair;"
Hands that plucked that faded rose
Moulder in their last repose.
Mirror mine! thou giv'st not me
Just the face I asked of thee;
Darker shadows cross the brow;
Lines of care are deeper now;

Heavier pulses heave the breast ;

Wearier spirit longs for rest.

Ponder this, O heart of mine !

Holier grow, as years decline

MY WESTERN HOME.

Softly lies the roseate glow,

On these Eastern hills of snow ;

Gaze I where the sun goes down,

On the hills of white and brown,

Thinking of my home away,

Neath that setting orb of day—

    My western home.

Stars unnumbered o'er me rise,

Fire-drops in the azure skies ;

One by one I miss their light,

From the diadem of night ;

Miss them with a starting tear,

For they seem to set so near

    My western home.

Morning brings her host of cares,

Lights her fires, and spreads her wares ;

Noontide comes with kindlier face ;

Winter smiles with kindlier grace ;

Here I grasp a friendly hand ;

Here I meet a cordial band,

　　But sigh for home.

I have pressed anew the sod

Where my infant footsteps trod ;

I have stood beneath the walls

Echoing once a mother's calls ;

Listening there I held my breath,

For the voices hushed in death—

　　Oh ! desolate home.

While I waited for the tones

Of the dear departed ones,

Living forms and voices came—

Living sisters called my name ;

Brothers of the heart said, " come !

Welcome weary wanderer home—

　　Come home, come home ! "

I have bent with reverent brow
O 'er a father's ashes now ;
I have walked with softly tread
Round a sister's narrow bed ;
But I love a baby's grave
Where the western forests wave—
    I must go home.

Hearts are there long known and loved—
Hearts by time and sorrow proved ;
Hearts that saw me fade and pine,
Like a rudely broken vine,
Seeming not to love me less
For my load of wretchedness—
    I will go home.

Mother may forget her child ;
Friends may frown who once have smiled ;
Trust may be repulsed with scorn ;
Love may plight her faith to mourn ;
But till memory's light shall set,
Never can my soul forget   .
    My western home.

"THE HEART WAS SO HOLLOW INSIDE."

I sat in a lady's parlor ;
 The lady was very fair ;
Silks rustled at every motion,
 And jewels gleamed in her hair ;
For she was a rich man's lady,
 And able such things to wear.

She sat embroidering worsted,
 In the sun's declining light,
And smiled on two rosy children,
 As she stitched in the scarlet and white,
The orange, and green, and purple ;
 And I thought it a beautiful sight.

But I heard a sound of footsteps,
 Of little, pattering feet,

Just as the wind was rising,

And the rain was turning to sleet;

And heard two wee-bit voices,

As the storm on the windows beat.

Then I heard the door bell ringing,

And ringing, and ringing, in vain,

And the tones of the wee-bit voices,

As I listened and listened again ;

And the harsh rebuke of a servant

Rang out through the icy rain.

Then those pattering feet came nearer ;

And close by the window was laid

A little white face, and round it

Bright curls of chestnut played ;

That face was hollow and hungry,

And the little white lips said :

" A small bit of bread, good lady,

For my little brother and me ;

We have *tried* to get work, but cannot ;

We are so *little*, you see,

That the men only laugh, when *we* ask them ;

Oh ! lady, so hungry we be !"

Then she lifted her eyes from the worsted,

Her smile giving place to a frown,

And her voice grew sharp and angry,

And she said, " Dirty beggar, begone !

Your fingers will mark the window ;

Get down, noisy fellow, get down !

Street beggars are troublesome creatures,"

She remarked, as her needle she plied ;

But, the beauty I worshiped had vanished,

For the heart was so hollow inside ;

I wondered if under all heaven

Was another so shrunken and dried.

I followed those sobbing children,

Away o'er the desolate moor,

Till their little blue fingers lifted
  The latch of their mother's door,
Where the rain beat down through the rafters,
  And froze, as it streamed o'er the floor.

I bent o'er her hard, cold pillow ;
  She whispered, "Oh! give them bread!"
And I answered, "God, help *me*, only
  As I stand in their mother's stead "—
With her heart's last throb she blessed me,
  Then want's poor child was dead.

THE CITY OF THE FLEAS.

I want to sing a little song,
   The country folks to please,
And make them happy where they are——
   A song about the fleas.

The rains were gone, the crops were in,
   And wife began to teaze
To see the city on the bay;
   She never thought of fleas.

" Take me, papa," said petted Kate,
   That romped beneath the trees ;
" I would be still and good—I would ! "
   She had not heard of fleas.

So down we went by stage and cars,
   Through dust that made us sneeze,

Took lodgings at The Grand Hotel,
   But never "ordered" fleas. - -

Wife bought a wig, a "Grecian bend,"
   And things to match with these,
And soon her trailing skirts began
   To gather in the fleas.

We walked, and rode, and felt as proud
   As any rich grandees;
Well pleased with all we saw—except
   The San Francisco fleas.

We went to "Woodward's Gardens," and
   Were happy, if you please,
But took a host of "bosom friends"
   We did not pay for—fleas.

We went to hear "Grace Greenwood" speak;
   I sat firm as a cheese,

Till stung " to death," from head to heel,
  By those terrific fleas.

I tried to be sublime, and soar
  Above low things like these,
When wife, within her crinoline,
  Whispered, " O dear! the fleas!"

' Papa!'" aloud screamed little Kate,
  " They're eating up my knees!"
And quick I bolted for the street,
  With family—and fleas.

We went *to see* " The Fourth of July,
  And faced a cutting breeze,
That whirled the sand about our ears,
  Peppered throughout with fleas.

We went to see all sights—all sounds
  That any hears or sees;

But memory's landmarks, slightly set,
  Are toppling o'er with fleas.

You may be rich, you may be great,
  But can not live at ease,
And share your sheets and pantaloons
  With half a million fleas.

Wife says to-day, "This dear old house,
  So cosy in the trees,
Is better than a palace in
  The City of the Fleas!"

8

"SOMETHING THAT WAS MY MOTHER'S."

Far in an eastern homestead,
   A thousand miles away,
Where an estate was settled,
   And came the "auction" day;

A tall man bore him proudly—
   The son executor;
The auctioneer was screaming,
   And all the crowd astir.

In lots were things assorted
   To give them speedier sale—
Sofas, and chairs, and tables,
   Bedding and linen pale.

All sorts of curious glasses,
   And delicate china ware,

Carpets, and quilts, and blankets,
　In deft array were there.

Naught was of latest fashion,
　But all unmarred and good ;
My duty was to purchase
　As cheaply as I could.

I stood before the china,
　Awaiting for its turn,
Attracted by some vases,
　And one neat breakfast urn.

I heard a voice behind me—
　A low beseeching tone—
Say, " Something that was mother's,
　One little vase or spoon."

I heard the surly answer :
　" The last thing shall be sold ;

Our father left you nothing ;
How can you be so bold ? "

" O, yes ! my angry father
Left all his wealth to you,
But I am still your sister ;
One angel loved the two.

" Something that was my mother's,"
She pleaded low again ;
" Some little thing of beauty,
Or this old counterpane."

And fast her bony fingers
Ran nervous o'er its flowers,
Their knotted outlines tracing,
As in her childhood's hours.

" Give me this one thing, Allen,
And I will go away ;

My mother died beneath it
  Five years ago to-day."

She opened wide its foldings ;
  She wet it with her tears ;
" Away ! " he sternly muttered,
  " How have you kept those years ? "

" I know I loved not wisely—
  But ah ! I loved too well ;
Please, something that was mother's—"
  The auction hammer fell.

" Stand back ! "   As Heaven is witness,
  A moment I was tried,
For I was there to purchase
  The outfit of a bride.

But, when her hand released it, .
  I only felt her pain,

And bought that sorrowing woman
  Her mother's counterpane.

Too full her thanks to utter;
  My outstretched hand she kissed;
And tearful neighbors blessed me,
  While "Allen's" name they hissed.

FALL OF THE CHARTER OAK.

Gone, ancient tree ! another cord doth sunder
  Which links affection to the hallowed past ;
No more beneath thy sheltering boughs we ponder—
  There 's naught so sacred but it falls at last.

Gone, forest monarch ! many a year ago
  The Indian hunter rested in thy shade,
On thy broad branches hung the winter's snow,
  And wind-rocked cradles with thy young leaves played.

We need not tell thy tale ; the little child,
  Taught by its mother, lisps it at the hearth,
How in thy bosom deftly lay concealed
  That Chartered Right which gave a nation birth.

How old wert thou when great Columbus sailed
  O'er the blue deep, hope in his bosom rife ?

How hath Tradition's misty record paled,

    Since in thy arteries waked the pulse of life !

King of the forest where the wigwam stood,

    Meet habitation for rude nature's child,

Where the brown maiden, mirrored in the flood,

    Shook her dark tresses at the waves and smiled.

Count us thy years : the hand of Time hath swept

    Thy forest brothers slowly from thy side ;

City on city into life hath crept,

    As westward rolled vast emigration's tide ;

While thou hast stood, in solemn grandeur still,

    With outstretched arms thy welcome mute to say,

And thousands gathered where thy shadows fell,

    Awed by the relic of a by-gone day.

No voice.　O man ! short-sighted, weak and vain !

    Mocked by the mystery of that ancient tree—

Thou only knowest, 'mid winds and driving rain,

    'T is crushed and scattered, and doth cease to be.

THE HUMAN BROW.

The human brow, the human brow !
  How cold, and calm, and white !
With passion's fire 't is glowing—now
  With virtue's holier light;
It wears the mystic web of care,
  The mystic sign of love,
The impress of untold despair,
  The seal of Heaven above.

Inscribed upon its arch sublime
  It wears a world of thought ;
The Day Book of relentless Time,
  'T is marred with many a blot ;
The lips may smile, the cheeks be dry,
  And tell no tale of grief,
The breaking heart may check the sigh
  Whose utterance were relief ;
    8*

But Nature's tablet still doth tell
  Where sorrow long hath dwelt;
Though lying lips proclaim, "'t is well,"
  The brow is marked with guilt;
Those stenographic words, so dim,
  Elude the careless gaze,
But Nature's student renders them,
  Through pride's concealing haze.

And he whose lips are moistened yet
  With sorrow's bitter dew,
Will know his "brother," and regret
  That record should be true;
Too well he knows the dismal sweep
  Of agony's cold pen;
And shuddering through his veins doth creep
  His own wild woes again.

That "brotherhood" of woe, alas!
  Grief's mute fraternity,

Unrecognized they come, and pass,

 As bubbles on the sea ;

Their dim " regalia " is not seen

 By men of happier mould ;

They meet, embrace, and part again,

 Till life's sad tale is told.

The human brow, the human brow !

 Most hallowed be its name !

O, sully not that sheet of snow,

 With the red brand of shame ;

Nor lines of grief, nor lines of care

 Its beauty can remove,

If " Purity " be written there,

 By *Him* whose name is " Love.

"I THANK THEM FOR THEIR SCORN."

I thank them for their scorn !
Had they not rudely on my heart-strings pressed
High thoughts, like these, that reign within my breast,
    Had ne'er of hope been born.

    Had they not coldly cast
Their deep contempt upon my mental powers,
I ne'er had dared to dedicate my hours
    To purposes so vast.

    I was a lonely child—
My fitful fancy wandering far away—
Though with my mates I shouted in my play,
    With footsteps fleet and wild.

    Visions of power and fame,
" Distant and dim," passed o'er my mental sight ;

My restless spirit panted for the might

    Of manhood's hardier frame.

    But when, at last, I grew

To manhood's stature, friends grew strangely cold,

And thought me foolish, confident and bold,

    Because *my* strength I knew.

    They claim the right, supreme,

To fetter down a free, aspiring mind,

By common rules its energies to bind,

    And bid it cease to dream !

    What ! quell the soul of man ?

Like the strong steed that fiercely champs his bit,

I scorn their power ; I can but stamp and fret,

    Till in life's battle van.

    Though I a beggar be,

O, soul of mine ! hold fast thy purpose high,

Till, firmly set in mind's imperial sky,

    Her stars acknowledge thee.

LETTERS.

I am going to write—and I " care not a straw "
    If I do meet the frowns of my betters;
For I know of no reason in ethics or law,
    Why I can't write a chapter on " letters,"
Those sweet little messengers, laden though light,
Which steal in like good angels, by day and by night.

I care not for the paper—its texture or hue,
    If it's rose-tinted, gilt-edged, or yellow;
If a stiff sheet of fool's-cap, all belted with blue,
    Or as soft as a peach when it's mellow;
I care not if it's written in " coarse hand " or " fine,"
If I see a friend's cognomen—and it is mine.

I care not if the writing goes zig-zag around,
    Like an awkward young ox when he's goaded,

I care not if it prances and flies o'er the ground,
    Like a restive young colt when it 's loaded ;
I care not if affection has blotted them there, ˙
If its commas are dashes—its periods nowhere.

But I care for its meaning—the face which it wears,
    Whose expression I only can render ;
For the heart which, unfettered by prudery, dares
    To write words for my reading so tender ;
For the heart, unsuspicious and truthful, that says
" I have loved—I do love—I will love you always."

I care not for beginnings—care not for the ends,
    If they come to me often and duly,
Though I think the epistles which pass between friends
    Should be closed with " I 'm yours," or " yours truly."
" Yours cordially,"—" faithfully,"—" ever " will do,
But " respectfully " never, *that* freezes me blue.

It will do for a dun, for a lawyer, a prude,
    For the man who by coldness would " cut " you ;

But I 'm sure between *friends* it is icy and rude,

   As if saying " with strangers I put you."

Oh ! the letter that 's simple, impulsive, and free

As a sun-beam from heaven, is the letter for me.

WHAT DO WE STRIVE FOR?

The longest life must end in death;

    What do we strive for here?

Fame also hath her living breath—

    Her last words and her bier;

Why spend our little inch of time

    In longing to be great;

Man's records are as pencilled rhyme,

    As figures on a slate.

Enjoy the flowers, aspiring fool!

    That deck thy youthful way;

At life's hot noon enjoy the cool

    Where shadowy fountains play;

When glimmering sinks life's western sun,

    Crave not its rise anew;

Rejoice! for weary nights are gone,

    And Heaven's sweet morn in view.

GREAT MEN NEVER DIE.

Where suns have set, a glory stays
    That lingers long behind ;
So memory floods, with hallowed rays,
    The western gates of mind.
The great man sleeps, but cannot die ;
    In all his works he breathes ;
The billowy years roll proudly by,
    Crowned with his laurel wreathes ;
And ages, with imperial sweep,
Still pass them on, from deep to deep.

THE DRAYMAN'S HORSE.

I will tell you a story.　Some years ago—

Fifteen or twenty—no matter now—

In a far-famed city—no matter where,

Nor how I, your servant, happened there—

A man was driving a poor old grey

In a crazy cart on the public way ;

He had trodden that pavement for many a year,

When the skies were black—when the skies were clear ;

Walking himself his horse to spare,

For "Pompey" he loved with affection rare.

Pompey was ancient and sadly worn—

His mane and tail had grown forlorn ;

His back was crooked, and low his head ;

His heels were heavy as lumps of lead ;

He seemed to be dropsical in his knees ;

His breath came forth with a pitiful wheeze ;

Oh ! he looked like a spider, made up of legs,

Or a poor old stick, driven full of pegs.

But a time is decreed for men to die,

And if not for horses, we wonder why ;

Poor " Pompey " had lived his time, and he

Lay down in his harness and ceased to be.

His master jerked and jerked the rein ;

" Get up old hoss ! " he cried in vain.

There he lay, like a log, in his olden tracks,

Undisturbed by the wheels of the passing hacks ;

While a traveler here, and a traveler there,

Turned aside from his errand to stop and stare.

One only mourner beside him wept,

While there in his harness, at rest, he slept.

Said his poor, old master in piteous tone :

" I 'm a beggar now, for my *hoss* is gone !

I have no home, nor friends, nor kin ;

Nobody will pity nor take me in.

Oh ! how shall I earn another cent,

For that poor old hovel, to pay the rent ;

And my dear old woman is blind and deaf;

Where—where in the world can I find relief? "

A murmur ran throughout the crowd;

Some whispered, "I'm sorry!"—some spoke aloud;

"Poor man!—alas! that the beast should die!"

(They needed but onions to make them cry;)

"Poor man!—poor soul!—what will he do?"

Was echoed by every comer new,

Till a thousand, or more, or less; had said:

"Poor man! I am sorry your horse is dead;

You had but *him* and that one old dray

To earn your living, from day to day;

There lies the horse, and the cart moves not;

Oh! sorrow and tears are our earthly lot."

Then I said in my heart—*I was younger then*—

"Each will give him a dollar to start again;"

But nobody whispered, "I'll give my part

Towards buying a horse to start that cart;"

Though their faces were long as rails, I ween,

And I wondered—*for then I was very "green!"*

"What *is* the matter?" a stranger cried,

And, thither and yonder, he pushed them aside;

" I see—I see—his horse is no more ;

His coat is ragged ; he 's old and poor ;

Look up, my friend ! I am sorry for you ;
Just fifty dollars—no thanks—adieu ? "

So saying, he left in his hand that sum.

The astonished crowd grew strangely mum ;

In another moment the ground was clear,

Nor moist where they stood with a single tear.

And I said in my heart, " Can this be real ? "

There were many to *speak,* but *one to feel !*

THEY WANT TO KNOW.

They want to know how old I am,
　　How long I have been married ;
If I have journeyed far and wide,
　　Or if at home have tarried ;
They ask me where I went to school,
　　And just how many quarters—
If I was trained with city belles,
　　Or 'mong the farmers' daughters.

They want to know about my shawl,
　　And where I found my bonnet,
How many yards, and what I paid
　　For all the ribbon on it.
They want to know how much I work,
　　And if it's profitable,
And if I use a silver fork
　　Or steel one, at the table.

They want to know about the man
    Who wooed my eldest sister,
They'd like to know how many times
    He visited and kissed her;
They want to know who tied the knot,
    A Methodist or Baptist,
And which of all that preacher's sons
    At learning was the aptest.

They want to know how long it was
    Before a crib was wanted,
And if the baby proved a girl—
    If "Pa" was disappointed.
They want to know if sister keeps
    A nurse and kettle-washer,
And if a mastiff churns her cream,
    Or if they use a dasher.

They want to know a thousand things
    I do not mean to tell them,

About the folks they 'll never see,

And all that e'er befell them.

I would I were a bird or bat,

I 'd fly away forever,

And hide me in some quiet nook

Where I 'd be questioned never.

9

HOW "TOM JONES" BECAME "MR. JONES" AND "THOMAS JONES, ESQ."

OR, "I'LL SIGN IF YOU'LL SIGN."

———

A TEMPERANCE STORY IN VERSE.

———

THOMAS JONES was a printer.   His youth promised fair
That his prime should be honored; the child of a pair,
Who were honest of heart and had taught him to go
In the safe path of virtue while dwelling below.

But the Demon INTEMPERANCE stood up in his way,
With his sword ready whetted his victim to slay.
"Come! come!" said he blandly; "there's pleasure with me;
I am king of the jovial, the happy and free.
Come drink of the nectar that foams in my bowl,
And the cares of the world shall sit light on thy soul;
Keen sorrow may sharpen its arrows in vain,
And whatever thy lot thou wilt scorn to complain;

The dark billows of change shall roll o'er thee unfelt,

And the storms of adversity powerlessly pelt

On the head I will arm with a helmet of steel,

For the friends of my bosom no anguish can feel."

Then he paused for an answer.

                          Deep buried in thought,

Tom reflected and doubted, yet answered him not.

He was thinking of lessons learned early in life,

Of his gray-headed parents and beautiful wife ;

Those parents who told him there was but one road

Led to happiness here, and hereafter to God.

And he thought of the maiden so happy and gay,

Who had turned from her father and mother away ;

Who had broke from her sisters, that artlessly clung

To her neck, when the parting words over them rung ;

Of the brothers who failed their keen anguish to hide,

When they left the last kiss on the lips of "the bride."

Then a smile curled the lip of the wily old fiend,

For he saw in this doubting no doubt of the end.

Lo! the man who doth *doubt* is already enslaved—
So the name of " Tom Jones " on his roll he engraved.

" Come and try me," he said, " thou wilt waste but an hour;
If my promise prove false, thou wilt still have the power
To return to the dull, plodding duties of life,
To remember thy parents and cherish thy wife; "
And poor Thomas reluctantly yielded assent,
And was led, like a blind man, wherever he went.

There was music and laughter, the wine sparkled bright;
There were savory viands on tablecloths white,
And bewitching companions of fashion and pride,
And he turned from the whisper of " *Home* " at his side.
There the night passed in riot, and chained to the spot
There the morning light found him, an embryo Sot.

A poor drunkard he lived, till his friends almost all
Ceased to think of him kindly, or mourn for his fall.
Only " Mary " yet loved him—his parents were gone—
And his drunken companions dropped off one by one;

Only "MARY" yet met him with smiles when he came,

And in accents of kindness repeated his name.

And as oft as there glimmered of reason a ray,

O'er the ruin RUM made him, he blessed *her* alway.

PETER CLARK was a merchant, well-known for his wealth,

For his foresight, and prudence, contentment, and health

Gave a glow to his cheek; tall, erect as a pine,

He drank nothing save water, tea, coffee or wine;

He drank wine, just enough to feel sprightly and well;

And he scorned those weak mortals who tasted *and fell.*

When old Alcohol's victims reeled into his store,

He arose—said, "Get out sirs!—sirs! there is the door!"

Now the "cold water" people at last were awaking

To a sense of their duty—the Rum-king was quaking.

They had spies on his movements, all true and alert,

Who were bribing his soldiers his flag to desert;

And they fought with his legions on mountain and plain,

In the streets of the cities, and ships on the main;

While the cowards who dared not change masters and fight,

In their hearts wished GOD-SPEED to the champions of RIGHT.

PETER CLARK in his counting room lingering alone,

Sat in silent reflection—clerks, customers gone.

All alone, did we say was our merchant to-night?

No, for CONSCIENCE was there in her terrible might,

" Thou ! " she said, " art the tree that dost cumber the
      ground,

And no fruit on thy branches forever is found ;

Thou dost keep thy own weaknesses snug on the shelf,

And despise thy poor neighbor, the pitiful elf;

Every man is thy brother ; no scorn in thy eye

Should repulse the poor drunkard who passes thee by;

Thou shouldst speak to him kindly, beseech him to hear

For her sake, who yet loves him, her children so dear.

Promise speedy redemption from suffering and shame,

And let *words* and *examples* be one and the same."

And the still voice of TRUTH gained a mighty control

O'er his habits of thinking—light came to his soul.

Then he thought of TOM JONES, and his pitiful plight—
Whom so often he 'd bidden " begone from his sight "
To his destitute wife and three famishing boys,
To distract her with curses, and scare them with noise.
And he thought of the " *pledge* " for such people " to sign,"
Which admits of " no brandy, nor whisky, nor wine."
Even JONES might be saved, were his name on the list,
And he thought he would ask *him* to " sign "—but, he 'd
    missed
Him some time from his door—what the reason could be,
He was quick to imagine, " some pitiful spree."

Hark ! a footstep—a heavy and blundering tread
Breaks the stillness of night ; and as people have said
Of the *Arch-Rogue* himself—who is sure to appear
When we 're thinking about him—so THOMAS is here ;
Not improved, but grown worse during absence, 'tis clear.

" Good e 'en, Mr. Merchant. The Temperance folks
Are all after me now with their ' pledges ' and jokes ;
They beset me so hard to go down where they meet,

That in running away I fell flat in the street.

But, thinks I to myself, 'I'm no turn-coat, not I;

I will drink what I please, and whenever I'm dry.

I have drank all my life, I am hearty and hale,

And I won't tack about now I'm under full sail.

I'm a man, though a drunkard, and minus a dime,

I have wallowed in gutters, but never in crime.'"

"Nay! nay! my good friend," said the merchant, "I think

'T is a terrible crime to indulge in strong drink;

And the 'Temperance Pledge' is an excellent thing,

The poor, wavering sons of temptation to bring

From the depths of delusion, to reason and right;

And I beg *you* will sign it—come, promise to-night!"

Thomas Jones straightened up; then he stroked his red
        nose,

Tied his mud-spattered kerchief, looked down at his toes;

Took his hat from his head, and adjusted the crown,

Which had swung like a gate on one hinge, up and down;

Shook his coat-skirt, all tattered, that trailed on the floor,

With the dirt it had gathered outside of the door;
Then, feeling his courage was up to the mark,
He replied, looking sternly in earnest at CLARK :

" Mr. CLARK, you might lecture an hour or a day;
I should know 't was all humbug—a scene in a play;
Let the wise man walk straight, and the fool lead along,
And not shout as *he stumbles*, ' hallo ! there; you 're wrong ! '
I am out of the turnpike, but you are there too ;
You leap over the mud, while I stick in the slough ;
You have wine at your dinners; I 've whisky, you see ;
You 're *too proud* to get drunk, and be caught in a spree ;
You would dirty your wrist-bands, so stiff and so fine,
And the crown of your hat would flip-flap just like mine;
You would scare all the ladies ; the dogs would all bark,
And the school boys would follow you *teazing ' old Clark.'*
How I wish *I could preach*—but, you asked me *to sign*—
When you write your own cognomen, scribble down mine.
But, good e'en, Mr. Merchant, quite sober I 'm growing,
I 've one friend who ne'er chides me—*to her* I am going."

9*

Now the sermon Tom preached was so pointed and true,

And presented in colors so clear to his view

The fact, that all lessons that aim at the heart

Should be backed by example—not taught as an art;

That he felt in his bosom an arrow lay deep,

And a conscience once troubled no longer could sleep.

"I will sign if you 'll sign" was not silenced nor hushed;

"If I 'sign' I may save him, so blighted and crushed."

It wailed in the night wind that lifted his hair,

It creaked as he rocked to and fro in his chair;

It was written in letters fantastic and tall,

Where the candle light flickered all over the wall.

He looked down at his watch—it was two hours past nine,

And he started for home; but, "I 'll sign if you 'll sign"

In the voice of his wife, ever happy and clear,

In an under-tone startled him—why was it *here?*

And the little feet pattering like mice o'er the floor

Said, "I 'll sign if you 'll sign,"—and repeated it o'er.

He retired to repose on a soft downy bed,

With a weight on his heart like a mountain of lead.

And no sleep o'er his senses stole gently and kind,

But a dream full of horrors affrighted his mind.

●

He dreamed he was walking, afar from the throng,

Where a beautiful river rolled sweetly along,

Through a flower-skirted valley that nestled between

Two mountains, whose summits were mantled in green ;

And the gray rocks hung o'er him, as vast and sublime

As eternity's arch o'er the Ocean of Time.

He looked up with reverence to HIM who had laid

Their mighty foundations, and thankfully prayed

That HE who had given *him* a path to pursue—

Where grandeur and loveliness gladdened his view—

Would help him to pity the lonely and sad,

Whose voices had ceased with their youth to be glad ;

Whose ways lay through morasses, deserts, and dells,

Where thorns grow profusely, and bitter the wells ;

Where the beast in his fury roams over the plain,

And the hot, heavy sand falls like pattering rain;
Where hope's last ray of light waxes faint and goes down,
And the wretched one doubts, and despairs, and is gone.

Lo! his path turned abruptly—a cottage was there—
And a shriek from its windows broke forth on the air.
'T was the shriek of a woman in peril of life—
And he sped to the spot—'t was the drunkard's poor wife.
'T was the wife of a demon, whom rum had made so,
And the husband, TOM JONES—was he aiming the blow.
The children, half starved, were all weeping around,
And his presence there only had stayed the death wound.
O Heaven! what wretchedness, hunger and dirt!
Some wrapped in old blankets, some lacking a shirt;
Their feet were all shoeless, their hair stiff and long,
And feathers and straws in its meshes held strong;
They stared at him wildly, then crouched down in fear,
For no stranger had entered their door for a year.
And their mother, whose spirit was crushed by despair,
Had ceased to watch o'er them with kindness and care.

"Stay—stay thy hand, ruffian! What! murder her now,

With the same hand that penciled this blight on her brow?

Remember! she trustfully gave thee her heart

In life's morning of gladness, unsullied by art;

In the pride of her beauty, surrounded by friends,

Thou didst swear to protect her—alas, how it ends!"

"I will sign if you'll sign," was the ready reply;

"If you will not, I'll drink till a drunkard I die."

He awoke with a shiver and turned on his bed—

There was dew on his temples and pain in his head.

"Oh! am I the man who is doing all this?

Is a hearth-stone by me robbed of plenty and bliss?

Lo! the wretch I might save from the horrors of sin

By a word of my mouth, and might easily win

From his dark, thorny path to the brightness of mine,

I thus leave to destruction, and cling to my wine.

God of mercy forgive me; I'll sign if he'll sign!"

Our merchant was seated again at his books,

Confused was his brain and perturbed were his looks;

He blotted his "ledger," mis-spelled and crossed out,
He wrote names so crooked they wheeled right about.
Mischarged and wrote, "Debtor to"—"*Sign if you'll sign*"
"Paid Mr. John Murphy"—"*No porter nor wine.*"
Then provoked at himself to be scared by a dream,
Though the very idea brought back that shrill scream,
He arose from his desk to gaze out on the street;
When along comes Tom Jones with his clattering feet.

Lo! his boot soles are loose and the leather is gone,
Till the school-boys have counted his toes every one,
As they chased him from corner to corner, *en masse,*
Crying, "Face about Captain, your sandals won't pass;"
His old beaver is flapping its wing in the wind,
And his neck-kerchief streams its long pennants behind;
His coat has quite lost its poor recreant skirt,
And displays his suspenders and tattered old shirt;
While the cuff of one sleeve is entirely gone,
And the other is ready to follow it soon.

"Any pipes, Mr. Clark? I'm quite sober you see.
Will you trust me? all others refuse to trust me.

While my money held out they were all very civil,

But they run from me now, like the saints from the Devil.

'There 's old Thomas,' they say, 'kick him out of the store.

Get away, you old brute ! ' they cry, shutting the door."

" Take a dozen of pipes ; you are welcome to-day

My good friend, MR. JONES ; glad to see you this way.

Let us go now, my brother, and write our names down

On the 'Temperance Pledge'—*both your name and my own.*"

" Agreed !" replied Thomas, " a liar I 'm not,

And no man from this hour shall call me ' a sot.'

Let us keep it a secret.   To-night I 'll go home

Just as straight as a deacon—*why thus I have come*

Will astonish my wife, and quite frighten my boys—

Who will miss all my cursing, and swearing, and noise ;

And my wife will conclude I am out of my head,

When she sees me go sober and quiet to bed.

I will do this a month, till she thinks me *quite mad,*

And in view of my ' craziness ' seems very sad."

" And when I shall have earned all that comfort requires,

For food and for clothing, for candles and fires ;

When my hat *like a man's* on my head shall be put,

And my hair on my temples be decently cut ;

When the last filthy rag shall be torn from my back,

And my boots leave behind them a gentleman's track ;

Then, then I will tell to my MARY the truth,

And her smile shall be glad as the smile of her youth."

And away went TOM JONES, and the merchant went too ;

And the people all laughed as the street they went through.

Such a contrast to see ; every window and door

Was now crowded with heads, as it ne'er was before ;

And they giggled, and shouted, and wondered, to see

" Such a gentleman going in low company."

MR. CLARK cared but little ; TOM cared not at all—

For they often had laughed at him when he did fall

In some gutter by chance, when his eyes had been dim,

And the boys had thrown stones and cried out, " Let him

　　　swim."

So they stared till they wearied ; and after all, when

They had half strained their eyes out, they only saw *men*.
And both did " sign the pledge. " And, as homeward they
    went,
They both felt the last hour had most wisely been spent,

From that hour THOMAS JONES never ceased from his work,
Though his former companions around him did lurk ;
Though his appetite craved for its portion again,
With a tear in his eye and a weight on his brain,
He wrought steadily on from the morning till night,
And was toiling anew at the dawning of light.

The benevolent marked him.   The case, they resolved,
Was " a case in which piety's self was involved."
They rejoiced, and encouraged with kindness the heart
In the pathway of duty now ready to start ;
They gave him employment, and cheered him with gold,
Paying more than he charged them—the half was not told.

Thus a month rolled away ; and his wife, as he said,
Was astonished to see him so early to bed.

The little ones played as he entered the door,

Never running to hide, as they 'd hidden before.

And his wife truly feared he *was crazed in his brain,*

As he went and returned ; went, and came yet again ;

Till the very last day of the time set apart

To keep secret his plan from the loved of his heart ;

Then with pockets well-filled, with the money to get

What would bring back the smile of his own Mary yet,

He set out on his errand, with pleasure and pride,

And first called at a tailor's.

                         " The grog shop 's that side,"

Said the tailor, alarmed lest some people might think

If he greeted him kindly, he too liked to drink.

" Have you ready-made clothing," he said, " Mr. Shears ?"

" Go away, you vile drunkard ! I 'll cut off your ears."

" Will you hear me ? " said Jones, looking right in his face,

" If I do n't get it here, I 'll try some other place.

I have money you see ! "—and his pocket he shook ;

Till the tailor amazed at the jingle did look.

" I have cash as you see, will you suit me or not?"

"Oh! walk in MR. JONES, I 've the best can be bought;

Here 's a vest, here a coat, here some pantaloons nice;"

And he said " MR. JONES " seventeen times and twice.

He took every thing down, with a bow and a smile,

Never wondering what people might think all the while,

And on tiptoe he walked, and he *walked very tall,*

As JONES tried them all on, and then paid for them all.

"You may send these," said Thomas—that tailor felt neat—

As he answered, "I will sir, to Washington street."

Next he went to a milliner's.   Walking right in,

He accosted a damsel, tall, pretty and thin.

" What 's the price of this bonnet?" when lo! how her

  cheeks

Turn the color of ashes, and hark! how she shrieks.

Then, recovering herself, she stands pressing her heart,

As if holding its fragments, all breaking apart.

" Did–you–ask–for–a–bonnet–sir?" gasping for breath.

"And which one?"

   "The white satin one, trimmed with a wreath.
What's the price of it?"

    "Price—sir—excuse me—three—four,
Just four dollars it is sir—I think it's no more."
"Well here is the pay, miss."

    "Pray where shall I send it sir?
Excuse me—I feared sir—pray do n't be offended sir."

"Well, my business," said he, as he entered the street,
"Is alarming the ladies, and all whom I meet.
I am dressed as Tom Jones, and wherever I come
They all think of '*delirium tremens*' and 'rum.'"

Then he went to the shoemaker's, buying boots there,
And of shoes for his family many a pair.
And the shoemaker, just like the tailor, received
Him quite coolly at first, till his soul was relieved,
Seeing money to pay for them; then he forgot
That "some people might see him chit-chat with a sot."

Then he purchased some goods of his friend MR. CLARK;

Then he went to a grocery—this brings us to " dark.",

And the grocer repulsed him till *cash* was revealed ;

Then on tiptoe *he* simpered, and balanced and wheeled,

Showing sugar, molasses, rice, coffee, and tea,

Saying, " please call again sir, you 'll know where we be."

Next he went to the meat shop—he boldly stepped in,

Though 't was long, very long, since a meat-block he 'd seen.

There two rumsellers stood, looking at him aghast,

As straight up to the butcher before them he passed.

" What 's the price of this round ? " said he, touching some
     beef,

As he thought of *how long* he had had none with grief.

" Beef ! beef ! ? " said the butcher, his jaws set apart

Till one might have gone down with a pony and cart.

" Beef ! beef ! ? " said the rumsellers—" beef ! did he say ?

Why the man is demented—he never can pay ! "

" Yes, beef ! " echoed Jones, " you all heard me I know,

Yet you all look amazed, as if I were a show.

What's the price of this piece?—come, my call must be
    brief.

Would you put me *in chains* when I ask you for beef?

Look here! I have money!" and flinging right down

A shilling, a dollar, a guinea, a crown,

Till he sprinkled the meat-block with money all o'er.

"There! there! do you see it—or must I show more?"

"Beef! beef!?" said the butcher—"Oh! beef sir you'd
    have.

Sir, I misunderstood you—what piece do you crave;

And where shall I send it, sir? Thank you—what name?"

"Why I have been 'TOM JONES'—I suppose I'm the same."

"Ah—yes! MR. JONES. William, carry this meat

Down to *Mister Tom Jones'* upon Washington street."

He was "*Mister Jones*" now. With a glance full of scorn

Such as makes a man "wish" he "had never been born,"

He accosted the rumsellers: "Sirs! do you see,

I've escaped from your mesh? Yes 't is really me.

Lo! the time is at hand when *your* '*beef*' will be scarce,

And your pockets be moneyless. This is no farce.

God is heeding the cry of the suffering poor

Who depend on the wretches who reel from your door!

May your wives and your children ne'er suffer for bread,

When the price of your wickedness lies on your head!

Now forever good-bye!—you 've a customer lost."

And for shame they were mute as the threshold he crossed.

We 've not named all his errands, nor where they were
    done;

He has traveled on briskly while lasted the sun,

And now twilight has found him enwrapped in her grey,

He is chatting, and bargaining, and paying away.

He has started for home; but before him, to-night,

Let us visit his cottage—yes, there is its light!

We 'll like good " Messmerees " make no noise by our call;

'T is the home of the poor, like the homes of them all.

Here are neatness and order through poverty seen,

And a something that tells of the days which have been;

And poor MARY, who sews for the shops at the stand,

Hath a face of rare beauty—a delicate hand.

Retrospection is busy ; how fixed is her gaze,

As she whispers, " I love him— I 've loved him always ! "

" Hark ! " she starts in surprise ; " some one knocks at the
       door."

Here 's a man with a cart and a barrel of flour.

" You are wrong sir," she says, with a tear in her eye,

"For we can 't buy wheat flour, the price is so high."

" I 've the pay in my pocket—I 'm right," said he then,

As he rolled in the barrel and started again.

Knock again at the door—boy and basket come in,

" Mr. Jones sent me here with these groceries for him."

Then he cast down ten papers at least at her feet,

And before she could answer, came boy with the *meat.*

" You 've mistaken the house, please to take them away,

For my husband I 'm sure is not able to pay."

" He has paid me already," each quickly replied,

As he left her to wonder, and hurried outside.

Tap again at the door—girl with bandbox has come.

" Is the lady of Squire Jones, Madam, at home ? "

" The lady ? " says Mary, and starts at the sound.

"I am Mrs. Tom Jones."

                  " Ma'am I 've brought you around

The new bonnet he bought of us ; please madam try it—"

" Are you sure it is paid for ? "

                " I am—let me tie it—

It is very becoming."

          "Ah ! yes, 't is I know—

But contrasts very strangely with garments below—

Such a bonnet as *this* looks too silly on me,

It was made for *some* lady, and mine cannot be !"

(Sweet Mary she sighed, for O, how could she guess

The right arm of her husband was bringing a dress.)

But the girl would not take it—'t was left on her head,

And she said, " If I 'm MARY JONES, reason has fled !

What a plight I am in with these bundles all here,

And that barrel, those boxes, all mine it is clear.

If by honesty earned, or benevolence given,

They are blessings direct from my ' Father in Heaven. ' "

" *You are Mary Jones, Mother,*" said Pet NUMBER ONE,

As he burrowed in bundles ; " I 'm glad they are gone,

For I smell in these papers both sugar and tea ;

We shall have warm white bread of that flour, won't we ? "

" Oh yes ! let 's have supper ! " said Pets Two and THREE.

At this moment Our Hero, too happy appeared,

And the mist from her mental sight readily cleared.

" Dear Thomas ! " " Dear Mary ! "

                    Here, reader, between

You and them falls the curtain, for here is a scene

Which our pen cannot paint you.   So, bidding all hail !

We shall leave with your fancy to finish the tale.

But we pray you remember, and ponder one line,

Where the moral all lies : " I WILL SIGN IF YOU 'LL SIGN."

"SPIRIT RAPPINGS," AS EXPERIENCED BY AN
OLD BACHELOR POET.

I was writing a song for the papers one night,
　All alone with my cat in an attic,
My cigar in full blast, and my feet left and right
　In a chair, for I 'm old and lymphatic;
And my hat on my head, for my hair 's thin and white—
　It was cold, and I 'm somewhat rheumatic.

I scribbled right on till my candle burned low,
　Not a mortal around me was stirring,
Not a whisper was heard, but some snoring below,
　And my tabby's own musical purring;
While the wind through the rafters was drifting the snow
　Which my window-pane gently was blurring.

My poem was finished—I sanded it o'er
　And leaned back with a long inspiration,

Saying, "weary old bachelor, scribble no more,

    Take your crust and your evening libation;"

When I heard little 'rappings' all over the floor,

    And I said: 'Is it fancy's creation?'

Then I saw in that attic, unpleasantly near,

    A light cloud, like a mist, gathering slowly;

And I said, " can it be that the 'rappers' are here

    To disturb one so peaceful and lowly?"

While I wished in my heart—though no mortal I fear—

    That my life had been somewhat more holy.

And denser and denser that shadow grew fast,—

    And a chilly sensation crept o'er me—

Intenser, intenser, till life-like at last

    It stood up on four feet right before me

But a wee little mouse—so the danger was o'er.

    Though I saw 't was determined to bore me.

Master 'Pussy,' awaking, sprang up as he saw

    What he thought a good supper to eat it;

But his foot passed right through it ; his velvety paw
  Clutched again, then he did not repeat it,
But drew back quite ashamed of that impotent claw,
  For no cat's in aforetime had beat it.

Now that little brown mouse op'es its wee lips to speak,
  Saying: "Master I crave your attention!
I'm a spirit, unhappy, that sympathy seek ;
  I entreat your profound condescension!"
Now it bows to me thrice, now is passive and meek,
  And I answer, "your griefs you may mention."

" But if you're a *she* spirit, get back by the wall,
  For I do n't allow feminines ever—
Though they hail from the shadow-land—near me at all,
  I'm afraid of their mischief forever.
If one passes my threshold and gives me a call,
  I get o'er the effect of it, never.

" I was once a mouse girl.   I was born in this garret,
  My birthplace a package of wool ;

My father and mother—I 'm proud to declare it—
　Oft said I was beautiful;
Yet my vanity needed not any should swear it,
　For I was not a particle dull.

" I could see my own ankles, elastic and slender,
　And my fur was as soft as a mole's—
I knew my own eyes were as brilliant and tender
　As were any that peeped from mouse-holes;
For I saw my own image ofttimes in the fender,
　When the boarder was gone from his coals.

" I attended mouse-school, where a mouse of position,
　A most dignified widow presided;
But I thought her a fool, whose profound erudition
　Made her petulant, thin and flab-sided;
And concluded no woman improved her condition
　By such lore as some mouse-men derided.

" I sat over the scraps from 'our boarders' epistles,
　And the bits from his books she 'd abstracted,

With my heart in the meadow of roses and thistles
    Which my-fancy had always attracted ;
But, I tell you I paid very ' dear for ' my ' whistles,'
    When she caught my attention distracted.   .

" From a box in this attic, I frequently toted
    A few leaves of antiquity's novels ;
On the hair-breadth escapes of rash lovers I doated,
    ' Seraphina's,' ' Malvina's ' and ' Lovels ; '
Upon ' underground passages ' fondly I gloated,
    Leading out to perfection in hovels.

" When I grew up to womanhood, graceful and witty,
    I was selfish as well as romantic ;
All the mouse-men around called me ' artless as pretty,'
    ' Not a particle proud or pedantic ; '
While I played the coquette—pray, sir, don 't look so gritty
    You 've worse humans both sides the Atlantic.

" Among all my lovers, one mouse-man came nearest
    My thought of a mouse's perfection—

He was handsome, a scholar, his head was the clearest,
    His voice had the sweetest inflection
When he said, 'will you wed me, my darling, my dearest?'
    I said 'I'll take time for reflection.'

"I 'took time,' but I never reflected, not I;
    'T was no part of my programme to think, sir,
And I flirted right on, like a gay butterfly,
    With the mouse-men that came at my wink, sir.
Oh, I liked to be flattered and told, with a sigh,
    I was 'sweet as a blossoming pink,' sir.

"When my lover grew restless, I called him 'capricious,'
    And he called me a heartless coquette, sir;
I replied—for to teaze him was very delicious—
    'I have twenty more fools in my net, sir.
Then he bade me 'good bye;' said 'you're lovely, but
        vicious,'
    And was gone, to my lasting regret, sir.

"Ne'ertheless, 'o'er spilled milk it is folly to weep,'
    So I married my wealthiest lover,

A grave middle aged rat, with a beautiful heap,
    As 't was ever my lot to discover,
Of provisions, and all things which rat nabobs keep
    In their store-rooms, but prudently cover.

" He was called ' Squire Rat,' and was highly respected
    By all rat-men and mouse-men around us ;
He was kind to me always, and no one suspected
    'T was a tie of convenience that bound us ;
But I wearied of him, growing daily dejected,
    And the spirit of jealousy found us.

" Then the tattlers began in his warped ear to tattle,
    Of a score of ' flirtations ' now ended ;
And he gave ' curtain lectures '—I tired of their rattle
    And the airs he put on when offended.
So I told him—lo ! out of it issued a battle,
    Which to breaking the marriage bond tended.

" He arose from his breakfast one morning, and said :
    ' Mrs. Rat I now leave you forever ;
      10*

I can't bear any longer such life as I 've led,

    And consider it prudent to sever.

Lo ! the homestead is yours, and the board and the bed

    I shall claim nevermore, madam, never !'

" He backed out of the hole, all his prudence withdrawn,

    When I heard the quick jump of a tabby

Which had watched round our premises evening and dawn.

    Oh ! that shriek !—'t was a murder most shabby !

There 's the rougue 'neath your chair, looking guiltily down,

    No wonder he 's careworn and flabby."

" Tabby " ventured no sign, but crept closer to me,

    As if craving protection in trouble.

" You vile murderer !" she said ; but no answer made he,

    For his conscience weighed more than a bubble ;

" It was cruel to him, and a pity you see,

    Since I never again was made double.

" Tabby missed of his feast—a poor rat passing by—

    He attempted to throttle and catch him ;

Now, I thought, is my time, with my strength I will try

  That poor corpse! through the door-way to fetch him.

So I stole him away while that battle ran high.

  O, ye stars! I did pull him and stretch him!

" We had a fine funeral; the service was read

  From the leaf of a prayer book, abstracted

From the stand of 'the boarder,' that stood by his bed.

  And I wept till some thought me distracted;   .

Then away from the grave I was tenderly led

  By our parson, so well I had acted.

" I mourned a whole week, refused comforts and calls—

  Quite a pattern of widowhood seeming,

Sat alone all day long in my desolate *halls*—

  None imagined of what I was dreaming.

Till my shadow one morning crept over the walls,

  As the sun through the door-way was streaming.

" I tripped over the meadow, as fleet as a fawn,

  In pursuit of my long absent lover,

Thinking now that the Squire was certainly gone,
   I would die, or my mouse-man discover.
So I journeyed all day, and all night, and at dawn
   There he sat 'neath a blossom of clover.

" 'Your obedient,' I said. 'Ah! my dear Mrs. Rat;
   Are you traveling for health or for pleasure?'
He replied most respectfully, lifting his hat;
   'Pray walk into my house, if you 've leisure.'
Ah! my poor weary heart! how it went pit-a-pat
   At the thought of recovering my treasure.

" But I followed him in to my grief and despair,
   For he said, 'Mrs. Rat, Mrs. Mouse, ma'am,'
As a lady arose, very stately and fair,
   Saying, 'pray be at home in our house, ma'am.'
Cataleptic I stood, gazing long on the pair,
   Then fell dead in the arms of the mouse-man.

" Looking back from the land where the mouse-spirits dwell,
   I saw mourning for me among mice, sir;

Mr. Mouse wrote at once to my friends how I fell,

    Then he buried me snugly and nice, sir.

But he shed not a tear, and I knew very well

    What had turned all his love into ice, sir.

" Get you back to the ghost-land of mice, perjured bride !

    I am tired of your feminine tattle "

" I won't go, Mr. Bachelor ! " pertly she cried,

    And I knew she was seeking a battle.

" You have humans as false, and as bitterly tried,

    Till the sands on their coffin lids rattle."

She tripped over the floor, coming close to my seat—

    " Down ! avaunt ! get you gone ! " I entreated,

But she sprang to my shoulder—slipped down to my feet,

    And anon on my hat crown was seated.

All my masculine wisdom was lost in defeat—

    Was e'er feminine wisdom defeated ?

How I wished for a monk to exorcise her down

    With good Hebrew and Latin instânter ;

But no monk was at hand, in his surplice and gown,

    And my courage decreased on a canter.

There was " Uncle Tom's Cabin " might " do it up brown,"

    But I'd lent it to Peter O'Shanter.

There was " Robinson Crusoe," " A Dream Book," " A

    Guide

    To All Countries by Land and by Sea ;

There was " John Helper's Crisis," " The Bandit's Fair

    Bride "—

    I read extracts from all like a bee.

Then a work on " Dyspepsia " and " Magic " I tried,

    But she clung all the closer to me.

I ransacked that library, moist with despair,

    And its shelves were all heavily lumbered ;

Saying : " Is there no volume so potent and rare,

    Of the mass with which these are encumbered,

As to banish this demon again to her lair ?

    If there's none, my last moments are numbered."

Then I took up those " Stanzas " last written, and read
    Them aloud in my wild desperation ;
" What is that ? " says Tormentor ; " a poem," I said.
    " That ! that ! it is nonsense ! vexation !
Stop ! hush ! I can 't bear it ! it murders my head ! "
    I replied, " you provoked the occasion."

Ere I reached the last " Stanza " I 'd writ for the papers,
    With a shriek she dissolved, (without Latin).
And I thought if all " rappers " that come to cut capers
    With old bachelors, perching their hat on,
Could but hear their " last lines," in the light of their tapers,
    They would melt from the beavers they sat on.

DOCTOR GRAY'S LECTURE ON PHRENOLOGY.

To a country town, not far away,

When the stage arrived, came DOCTOR GRAY—

Quite a handsome man in a suit of black—

So of course a "doctor" and not "a quack."

But no one questioned, and no one cared

How "the Doctor" looked, nor how he fared,

Till the bills were up at the hour of THREE,

Which " A LECTURE " announced "On Phrenology."

At early SIX the world is there;

The fire blazes, the candles flare,

And "DOCTOR GRAY," unabashed and free,

Harangues the crowd on "PHRENOLOGY."

"There are 'heads,' he said, "of a wondrous size,

And such are the 'heads' which are wondrous wise;

There are 'heads' of the medium size we know,

Which must move in the common sphere below;

And some 'heads' there are, in this world of ours,

Of diminutive size and contracted powers.

As 'heads' differ in size, so they differ in shape,

And man differs from man, as does Man from the Ape."

Then he turned to the portraits of WEBSTER and CLAY,

And CALHOUN, POLK, and JACKSON, hung up in array.

"Mark the difference twixt those God created to rule,

And the low shallow pate of this cast of a fool."

Then the boys clapped their hands, and the boy-headed men

Rang the walls with their laughter, again and again.

"All the fools are like fops," he said, low with a wink,

"Having self-esteem larger than organs that think;

And one organ unbalanced, hangs backward you see,

Like a nest full of wasps on the limb of a tree."

Then he spoke upon SEXES; and straightway made out

That the males dress in jackets, the females without.

That the males go to battles, elections and races,

And the females tend babies at home, in their places.

And along he proceeded through all that he knew,

And much more that he *knew not*, before he got through.

And the audience, grown weary, began to be showing

They were sorry they came, and meant soon to be going.

For he blundered, and wandered so far from his text

That they wondered what subject he 'd stumble o'er next ;

And remarked, as they viewed him 'mong portraits and
      skulls,

That some *lectured on brains*, who were consummate gulls.

But, before very desperate they ran to their beds,

He proceeded to say, " We 'll examine some heads."

Then the company seemed in a little commotion

As they chose a few " Heads " from humanity's ocean ;

And the persons selected went forth for inspection,

Like a bevy of rogues in the way of detection.

There were twelve in the number—one preacher, one lawyer,

One judge, and one poet, one common wood-sawyer,

One butcher, one fiddler, one mathematician,

One " Mrs. McMurphy "—not born a patrician—

A woman of letters, " Miss Deborah Hearty,"

A sweet little linguist, " Miss Flora Mc Carty,"

And my own *modest self*—now excused from the party.

A moment of silence succeeded the hum,

The children, admonished, sat perfectly mum.

Then, up-raising his eye-brows and straining his eyes,

Till he looked like a screech-owl—he talked in this wise.

" Here 's a man," said he, touching the reverend brow

Of the pious old MINISTER, " I must put low,

On ' reflection,' ' perception,' and ' morals ' you see,

For his forehead slopes back like the curve of a D.

His ' benevolence ' and ' reverence ' I find very small ;

I much doubt if *this gentleman* worships at all.

But I find his ' constructiveness ' pretty good size,

And both ' color ' and ' form,' which are over the eyes.

He might plan him a cottage, and build it, and paint it,

Though I fear he with purple or yellow might taint it."

Then he listened for laughter—no laughter was there—

And he said, " I am done with him," smoothing his hair.

When *his reverence* remarked, with a smile on his face,

" After forty years' preaching, behold ! my disgrace."

Then he turned to the lawyer.   " This man hath a brain

Of unusual dimensions—I hope he 's not vain—

And this man I infer is a man of some wit,

If this man be a lawyer "—"He's hit *him*, he's hit!"

Said the boys, while "the doctor," not seeming to hear,

Went ahead with a spring like the bound of a deer.

"I say, ladies and gentlemen, though I do n't know,

If a lawyer, I pity *his* litigant foe;

On the 'moral' and 'social' I find him not large;

May be kind to a lady, if left in his charge;

He is bold and satirical, cautious and sly;

He's an orator—look at that prominent eye!

He is one who looks out for his client and dimes;

He takes care of himself—'t is a trick of the times."

"Very good!" said the audience—*who did n't say "fudge."*

Then he laid his white hand on the brow of the judge.

"This good man has a 'head,' which 't is plain to you all,

Is of medium size, and an intellect small;

His 'perception,' 'reflection,' and 'morals' range low,

And his 'temperament' is 'sanguine' and 'bilious' you

　　know.

If a journeyman tailor, or grocery clerk,

I should think he might be very brisk at his work."

Then he listened again, and a murmur was heard

From indignant observers—"absurd!—how absurd!"

For "the judge" was considered the wisest of men—

They revered him before, and they reverenced him then.

And the doctor discomfited—rather than show it—

Hurried on to examine the head of—our Poet.

"This young man," said he, looking him full in the face,

Has an intellect large, as I readily trace."

And his fingers went off at a galloping rate

O'er the hights and the hollows of Poetry's pate.

"'Calculation' tremendous—'causality large,'

And a 'memory' that holds all he puts in his charge;

Low on 'Time' and on 'Tune'—he is not a musician—

I should think this young man is a mathematician;

I will venture to say that this man may live long,

And make many a figure, but never a song."

There was laughter aloud—he supposed at his wit—

But they laughed that "the shoe was so far from a fit."

Then he passed to the wood-sawyer.   Here let us say
That "Bill Cutter" was dressed like a beau in a play ;
And his "head" was a Webster's, if judged by its size,
And his face was a fine one, with shiny black eyes ;
While the hands *in the* told no tale of the saw—
Hence the doctor proceeds his conclusions to draw.

" I should think that this man might be known in the town
As a person of talent—this man is no clown.
He 's a writer perhaps—yes, a poet, I see :
' Ideality's large,' and the ' marvellous ' has he,
And of 'Time,' 'Tune,' and 'Language,' a wonderous degree.
Yes, here *is a scholar*, who oft as he chooses,
Can write tales of romance, or converse with the Muses."

" Look here Mr. Doctor ! " indignant, said Bill,
" If you call names in Latin, I 'll flog you, I will !
I'm a sawyer of wood, and I earn my own clothes,
But take care what you call me—or look to your nose ! "
And amid the wild laughter, provoked by his speech,
Master Bill, homeward bound, ran away out of reach.

Next in turn came THE BUTCHER.   He made him out simple

As a sweet little girl with a smile and a dimple ;

Or the sensitive lady who weeps oe'r the "pullet"

She has ordered for dinner, deploring the "bullet."

Then he tried the musician, and left " him no Tune ; "

And "no time " and no brains, like a pitiful loon ;

Though all knew he had intellect, brilliant and rare,

'Neath that glossy profusion of chestnut-brown hair.

Now the MATHEMATICIAN was called to his doom—

And again those sage fingers swept on like a broom.

" This is one of those persons we meet every day

In life's commoner walks ; never born for display ;

With no talent which precedence takes of the rest—

This man likes that his dinners should be of the best ;

And will pass through the world like the mass of mankind,

Undistinguished for anything—medium mind.

He has musical genius—good man," said he winking,

" Give him plenty of money, he 'll *hire his thinking.*"

And with this he dismissed Mr. Charley Division,

And the walls echoed then with the laugh of derision.

And he laughed with the rest, thinking wit and good gues-
    sing,

To a lecturer on brain were a help and a blessing.

Next was Mrs. McMurphy, unlettered and bold,

He pronounced her " a lady of delicate mould ; "

Bade her " cultivate flowers ; take care of her health

Lest her mind should out-weary her body by stealth."

And her bluish white eyes gave a satisfied stare

As she yawned, like a clam—then she slept in her chair.

Next examined—" Miss Hearty," an author and belle,

He allowed her " scarce talent " to " *cypher* " and spell ;

Just enough to tend babies and worship her spouse,

And look after the servants and webs in her house.

" My true character ! " answered the roguish Miss Hearty,

Then he passed to the linguist, sweet " Flora McCarthy."

" Hem ! ahem ! ! " said the doctor ; " the less that is said

Very often's the better.   A nice little head,

And its owner a peaceable gay little girl,

Who thinks less of a book than a feather or curl;

And is oftener seen at a ball or a play

Than at lectures on science—what more need I say.

May I hope the kind audience is satisfied now?"

And the rush for the door left no room for his bow.

We scattered like pigeons, and flew to our nests,

To have nightmare and skeleton skulls on our breasts.

II

RETRIBUTION.

Fast toiling up a sloping mound
  On which a mansion towered,
A woman in a muslin robe
  Before a tempest cowered.

She stopped before a massive door
  Of neatly carved device,
And there she knocked and knocked again,
  And then repeated thrice.

The servants knew her sad, pale face,
  But dared not bid her in,
Though pained to see her look so poor;
  Who had their favorite been.

"I will go in!" she said; "he can
  But hurl me to the street;

He can but spurn his suffering child,

 And drive her from his feet.

" O father! round my darling's form

 Death twines his chilly arms;

Forgive him, that he loved me, now

 No life his bosom warms.

" Grant me a trifle of thy wealth

 To ... his funeral rite,

And Heaven will increase thy store,

 And bless thee for the mite.

" Oh! in that day when all shall meet,

 And at one bar appear,

Can Mercy spread her shielding wing

 O'er one that mocks her here?"

And still she wept, and still her sire

 Looked on in cold disdain,

And bade her "go! nor seek his face,
  Nor shade his door again!"

"I go," she said; "no daughter's curse
  Shall linger from my tongue.
May such a weight as crushes mine
  Ne'er on thy soul be hung!"

She went, and asked of strangers the
  Her starving children's bread;
And christian strangers bought a shroud
  And coffin for her dead.

That heavy sand—that heavy sand
  Upon the coffin lid!
It seemed to strike her bosom, too,
  And tear it as it slid.

But duller, heavier grew the sound
  Of rattling earth and spade,

Till, beating down the new brown grave,
 The kindly work was stayed.

Then, sadly toward her desolate home
 She led those babes away,
As, sinking neath the western hills,
 Went down the Orb of Day. .

There was a form that lingered yet
 That breaking mass behind ;
A stranger he, whose dress and air
 Bespoke the man of mind.

A few white hairs his temples wore,
 Inwoven with the brown,
And sorrow on his cheek had traced
 Her lines too plainly down.

Yet kindness lingered on his lip,
 And mercy in his eye,

For Heaven had penciled beauty there
    In lines that could not die.

Closely he followed now the steps
    Of that fair group of three,
Answering their first inquiring glance
    With : " Mourners, fear not me !

" I am a helper, sent to ye
    From every widow's GOD ;
His falling mantle clings to me,
    Who lies 'neath yonder sod.

" Come to my heart, poor, stricken one !
    Child of my early love ;
A father I will be to thee,
    Or loose my crown above !

" O Imogene ! thy mother sleeps
    Beyond tyrannic power ;

Breathed *she* one name unknown to thee,
    In any thoughtless hour?

" Child ! did her bark glide smoothly on,
    Unrocked by sorrow's tide,
  Until her life-sun calmly set
    Behind the hills of pride?

" Gave she to him who held her hand
    An undivided heart?
  Or did one Image haunt her soul,
    Refusing to depart?

" My daughter ! there is no remorse
    To feed thy sorrow's bowl ;
  Thou didst not send thy lover forth
    With arrows in his soul."

" Ah ! mine is but a selfish grief ! "
    She wiped her tears and said ;

"I will devote my life to thee;
With God I leave my dead.

"There *was* a name my mother called
When struggling hard with Death;
With that dear name upon her lips,
She yielded up her breath.

"Edwin!" she said, "I love thee yet!
God keep thee through the world,
While tyrants o'er the human heart
Shall to the dust be hurled."

They say she raved—her broken words
I gave to memory;
And lo! this hour reveals to me
Their all of mystery.

Sweet Imogene and her's no more
Were in that valley seen;

And winter came, and spring returned
  With all its bloom and green ;

And summer passed ; and years rolled on ;
  Yet still her sire was here ;
His goods increasing with his years,
  And every blessing near.

His locks but slowly bleached to gray ;
  No wrinkles marred his cheek ;
The fool forgot that God is great,
  And man, the creature, weak.   .

But Justice doth not always sleep,
  Though sometimes long delayed.
Around the Sinner's hopes, at last,
  Flashed the avenging blade.

A blight destroyed his waving fields ;
  His cattle strangely fell ;

Men would no longer work for hire,
  Where lay a curse's spell.

Alone, beneath his stately roof,
  He lived, an outcast now;
While lightning burned his spacious barns;
  Wind laid his fences low.

The borrower returned him not
  The money he had lent;
And bankrupt houses failed to pay
  The wonted yearly rent.

No eye of pity wept for him,
  None marveled at his fate;
All said, "the flaming sword of Wrath
  Swept over *him* too late."

How could he breathe amid the scorn
  Of those despised so long?

Or he, who ne'er forgave a fault,
    Bow to confess a wrong.

The pride that ruled his better days
    Yet clung to his despair,
And sent him forth to distant lands—
    None asked the question, " where ? "

———

Upon a city's pavement lay
    A shadow broad and tall,
Which from a princely mansion fell—
    A princely student's hall.

A lady at the window stood
    To view a passing show ;
When lo ! upon her marble steps
    She saw a form of woe !

A beggar ! weary, worn and old,
    With deeply sunken eye ;

And strangely did her bosom heave,
　　To hear his plaintive cry.

Her every pulse was charity ;
　　Her feet obeyed her heart ;
When to the door she quickly sped,
　　To act the Christian's part.

" Come in ! come in ! " she sweetly said,
　　" And tell to me thy grief ;
Come, I will bathe thy aching head,
　　And give thee sweet relief.

" Come ! let me smooth those hoary locks,
　　And wipe away thy tears ;
I 'll strive to make thy soul forget
　　The wrongs and ills of years.

" Say, are they dead who loved thee long,
　　Or far estranged from thee ?

Come in ! thou aged pilgrim, come
　And tell thy tale to me !

" Come ! God hath given me of wealth
　　Abundance, and to spare ;
Mine shall be thine—stay—all thy days
　In all my blessings share."

Why did his feet refuse to cross
　The threshold of her home,
Though she had taken his cold hand—
　And still she bade him, " come ! "

His eyes were fixed upon her form—
　He quailed beneath her look ;
And every stiff and weary limb
　With deep emotion shook.

Well might he shrink ; before him stood
　The child he spurned in pride ;
" Forgive me, Imogene ! " he gasped,
　And on her threshold died.

THE THREE BRIDES.

[The plot of this poem was suggested by the short prose story of F. L. Durivage,
with the same title.]

An old man stood a grave beside
  And leaned upon his spade,
Another child of dust and pride
  Beneath the turf was laid ;
Soft zephyrs played amid his hair—
  Upraised it from his brow,
Or left his hollow temples bare,
  Then veiled them with the snow.

His eye was dark : it told of dreams,
  Of deep unuttered thought ;
It lighted up with fitful beams,
  As from a heart o'er wrought ;
It cast a mournful glance around,
  It lingered on the wall,

It rested on that new-made mound
    Crossed by his shadow tall.

" Father," I said, " thy cheeks are white,
    Thy lips are thin and pale,
Thy locks are as the dews of night,
    Or as the glittering hail ;
Thy brow is seamed with marks of care,
    Thy stately form is bent;
Forgive me, if I ask thee where
    And how thy years were spent ? "

A searching look he turned on me,
    And answered : " Grief is old ;
My counted years are forty-three,
    When all my years are told.
Boy, wouldst thou see the blackened trace
    Of God's avenging doom ?
Come where he hid his mercy's face
    And sealed a soul to gloom."

Then turning from that grave so new,
  With quick, impulsive tread,
He passed the arching gateway through,
  Whose walls enclosed the dead.
I followed as he rushed along—
  That bent and white-haired man—
As if his limbs again were strong,
  And youth returned again.

Past meadow, marsh, and streamlet clear,
  And waving grain we sped ;
The village lessened in our rear,
  The mountains rose ahead ;
Yet, beckoning still, he hurried on,
  His lips in silence bound,
Till, centered in a velvet lawn,
  A silent home we found.

He pointed to its towering walls
  Against the cloudless sky,

And said, " no sound disturbs its halls
    Besides the cricket's cry."
The wind its shrunken shutters flapped,
    The doors were loose and wide,
The shingles on the rafters tapped,
    And moss o'erspread its side.

" Come in," he said, and through my blood
    A chill sensation crept,
When on its floor the old man stood,
    And I beside him stept.
For oh ! the scene that met my gaze
    Was fearful, sad, and strange ;
It told a tale of other days,
    Some dark, mysterious change.

Rich drapery, from the ceiling hung,
    Had faded all to gray ;
A harp, neglected and unstrung,
    Dust-wrapped and voiceless lay ;

The woolen fabric 'neath our feet
　　The moth had half consumed ;
Across the damask table-sheet
　　The spider's web was loomed.

And many a noble volume there
　　The mouse had made her jest,
And works of art, the rich and rare,
　　The mould of time had dressed ;
The damp had silver vessels dimmed,
　　The brass were black with rust,
The lamps burned out, and ne'er retrimmed,
　　Were pyramids of dust.

"Why is it thus, my guide ? " I said,
　　" Here desolation reigns ;
Can'st thou remove this mystic dread
　　That creeps throughout my veins ?
Tell now to me the gloomy tale
　　Of this abandoned home,

Before the setting sun-beams pale
   On yonder temple's dome."

" Sit down," he said, "sit down, I pray
   I fain would tell thee all ;
Here glide no ghosts, as cowards say,
   When night's deep shadows fall.
I would we heard óne gentle sigh,
   One low, familiar tone,
Or felt the unseen passer-by,
   Loved and forever gone.

" I would there were white wings around,
   Which only I could see,
That voices of unearthly sound
   Would sing for only me.
But now I turn for thee the leaf
   Which ne'er was turned for man—
Forgive this timeless burst of grief."
   And lo ! the tale began.

"Tired of the world, its empty joys,
  Its fashions and its cares,
A student left its glare and noise,
  Unfettered by its snares.
He reared these walls, content to hide
  In nature's shades to rest,
With one fair child, his hope and pride,
  A frail, dependent guest.

" Here, to his home he luxuries brought
  For this his only son ;
Though for himself nor craved nor sought—
  They pleased his precious one,
Who wore his sainted mother's smile,
  And shook her clustering hair ;
Sighing, he smoothed his locks the while,
  And blessed her image there.

" ' Thou art my only tie to life,'
  He kissed him oft, and said,

' Dear semblance of my gentle wife,
 My beautiful, my dead !
For her sweet sake I cling to thee,
 Cling thou to her above ;
Ne'er let that angel mother see
 Her child beneath her love.'

" On swept the years ; that gentle boy
 To manhood swiftly grew ;
His hopes were shared, his every joy
 That faithful father knew.
The varied works of ancient lore
 He to the child made plain,
O'er all the heights he'd climbed before
 He led his charge again.

" Death claimed his own ; the good man died ;
 The son could only weep,
And lay him by his mother's side,
 To share her peaceful sleep.

But oh ! the aching loneliness
    That o'er his spirit stole,
When none was left with love to bless
    His young and yearning soul.

" Yet grief its first keen edge must lose—
    We cannot always mourn—
The rod foregoes its power to bruise,
    When long its stripes we 've borne.
Ambition called, he sought a name—
    To write a name unknown
Upon the highest towers of fame,
    And grave it on her throne.

" He wooed the muses; for the fire
    Of poesy he felt,
And seldom with the mystic lyre
    Such harmony had dwelt.
In far-off lands his name was heard—
    There many a household band,

Aroused to deeds of love deferred,
    Blessed his inspiring hand.

" Men said, ' Behold ! the youthful sage
    Is prince of modern bards ;
He pens for us the fairest page
    The present age records ! '
The smiling lip, the laughing eye,
    Of beauty seemed to say
She must be blessed, who by-and-by
    Shall steal his heart away.

" Where yon tall cedar proudly towers
    Against the arching blue,
Three sisters spent those guileless hours
    When life and love were new ;
All graceful as the angel forms
    That come to us at night,
And hold us in their peaceful arms
    Till breaks the morning light.

" Helena was the youngest child,
   The rose-bud of the three ;
Her statelier sisters paused and smiled
   To hear her bursts of glee—
As bounding like the sportive fawn
   She crossed the native heath,
Or wove for each a flowery crown,
   Their loftier brows to wreath.

" Her heart the poet won, she gave
   To him her priceless hand ;
' My own ! ' he said, ' to shield and save
   From error's rock-browed strand.'
' My own ! ' how wildly leaps the heart
   When first we say ' my own '—
With quivering lips and tears astart—
   ' My own—my blessed one ! '

" Imploring Heaven the bond to bless,
   The father gave the bride ;

The mother gave the parting kiss
With less of grief than pride ;
The sisters then their darling clasped,
With blessings on her head,
And all was o'er—the pageant passed—
Away the bride was led.

" Helena ! how the flowers up sprung,
And choked the weeds of care ;
The poet, listening to thy song,
Forgot his harp was there ;
The garden gathered new perfume
Beneath thy fostering smile ;
From path to path, from bloom to bloom,
Enchantment reigned the while.

" But joy possessed is half decayed ;
We grasp it—it is gone !
Death, with his ruthless sickle, laid
That flower of virtue down.

12

He loosed her from reluctant arms,

That sweet confiding vine,

Content to wreath her artless charms

Around his household shrine.

" Yet time assuaged his bitter grief—

The heart is prone to change ;

To make my truthful story brief—

Though seeming wondrous strange—

He sought the second sister's heart,

He claimed a second bride;

Death, envious, sent another dart,

And swept *her* from his side.

" Edwina ! she was pale and meek,

Pure as an angel's sigh,

White lilies rested on her cheek,

And kindness in her eye.

She listened to the lightest call

From pleading misery ;

From wealth to want, beloved of all,
  All mourned her destiny.

" Why go our whitest lambs so soon
    From out affection's fold,
  While spotted Vice enjoys her June,
    Her Autumn, and grows old ?
  But time again brings healing balm—
    A slow, imperfect cure—
  The stricken man is peaceful, calm,
    And stronger to endure.

" Lo ! queenly Caroline is there,
    The eldest sister lives ;
  Tall, graceful, and supremely fair,
    She wins him as she grieves.
  He drinks her eyes' bewitching light,
    And mind replies to mind,
  She claims him with imperial right,
    To captivate and bind.

" With brilliant lamps the chapel gleamed,
　　Its pillars wreathed with green,
The lustre all around her streamed
　　Who stood a bridal queen.
White roses twined the locks among,
　　Which waved around her brow,
And o'er her matchless shoulders hung,
　· Contrasting with their snow.

" The organ pealed with solemn sound
　　A prayer—a reverent pause—
The bride was given—then all around
　　Was low, suppressed applause.
The bridegroom spoke the vows with pride
　　He purposed to fulfill ;
Then sweetly said that lovely bride,
　　In low response, 'I will.'

" But scarce from off her lips the sound
　　Had calmly died away,

When terror seized the circle round,
  And trembling and dismay.
There came a flash, a bright red flash,
  A loud, unearthly wail,
The pillars shook amidst the crash
  Of thunder, wind and hail.

" The fair ones shrieked ; the bride alone
  Was equal to the hour,
She made response in louder tone,
  Nor feared that tempest's power.
No quiver of her lip betrayed
  One shrinking pang within—
He thought her calm and undismayed
  Because so free from sin.

" The rite was o'er—the moonbeams fell
  On glittering bower and bush ;
The guests dispersed, the tale to tell
  Amid the household hush.

Again the bridegroom to these walls
  A worshiped mistress led ;
Yea, brought her to these fretted halls,
  Now sacred to the dead.

" But lo ! a second cloud doth rise ;
  It shrouds the moon and stars ;
The lightning o'er its surface flies—
  The earth with thunder jars.
' Hide thee,' he cries, ' my love, my bride !
  Within our sheltering home ;
Hide thee ! its portals open wide—
  Hide from the outward gloom.'

" They yet upon the threshold stood ;
  ' Go in ! ' he cried in vain ;
The hail, the thunder, and the flood
  Swept over hill and plain ;
A flash of fiercer, redder dye
  Lit up the darkened air,

It lingered in her large, full eye,
　　And burned amid her hair.

" ' I may not cross thy threshold now,'
　　In husky whispers came ;
' Thou seest upon my burning brow
　　God's own avenging flame.
　My tongue is parched, my eyes are dim,
　　My veins are all aglow ;
　And lo ! I pass away to Him,　　　．
　　Consuming as I go.

" ' 'T was I that drugged with poison deep
　　Each trusting sister's bowl ;
　Then mourned with thee her timeless sleep—
　　Lost and degraded soul !
　But oh ! 't was love—'t was love for thee,
　　Concealed within my breast—
　That nerved my arm for infamy—
　　A demon of unrest.

" " 'T was love, the unreturned and true,
    That drove me to despair,
And maddened—lost—a fiend ! I slew
    The lambs that claimed my care.
Helena ! with what earnest love
    My bending neck she clasped !
Edwina ! pure, confiding dove,
    Dying, my fingers grasped.'

" He.could not curse, he dared not bless
    His lost and guilty bride,
There, shorn of all her loveliness,
    Still clinging to his side.
He gently loosed her pleading hands,
    And whispered : God is just ;
But Jesus feels and understands
    The sorrows born of dust.

" A costly tomb received her form,
    And wandering Rumor said,

She perished in the fearful storm
  That beat upon her head.
They said she perished like a flower
  Crushed by the water's weight—
Soared Heaven-ward 'mid that fearful shower,
  And left a cheerless mate.

" He turned away—yet naught revealed—
  To hope and smile no more ;
With forehead bowed and bosom sealed
  His lonely lot he bore.
What now to him was wealth, or fame,
  Or love's delusive dreams ?
He sought not power, he feared not shame,
  But sighed for Lethean streams.

" Forgetfulness ! in vain thy wave
  He prayed to haste and come,
While onward to the peaceful grave
  He bore the weight of gloom.

12*

Vile slander, with her scorpion tongue,

 At last his name defiled,

But all too late her darts were flung

 At sorrow's wasting child.

" His home, enwrapped in dust and mould,

 Is yielding to decay ;

Yet here till life's last hours are told

 He will return to pray.

What wonder if his spirit clings

 To haunts where grief doth sleep,

And here the friendly dust he flings

 O'er hearts no more to weep."

" And thou art he indeed, my guide—

 Whom fate so strangely led—

The poet, and the man of pride,

 On early flattery fed ;

The husband of the fated three—

 Each loved and gifted wife—

Oh ! vain is weak philosophy
To stem the ills of life."

" Away ! away ! I 've told thee all—
Nor stay to see my tears—
For thee I 've let the curtain fall
Which hid the woes of years."
I left him there, again to tell
His woes to Sorrow's Friend ;
And thought, Life's Drama, opening well,
Oft brings a Tragic end.

THE BATTLE FIELD.

Rest, soldiers, rest !   The earth is damp
  With many a comrade's blood,
Who faltered 'mid the battle's tramp,
  And perished while ye stood ;
But fainting nature pleads for sleep ;
No time is yours to search, or weep
  For lost ones on the road.

Rest, soldiers, rest !   May angels guard
  Your slumbers as before ;
Bring home's green vines by south-winds stirred,
  And rose-trees from the door.
The gentle mother's low " good night "—
Sweet wife and children treading light—
  The homestead's hallowed floor.

The weary slept ; the wounded turned

   To sunlight's fading glow ;

Oh, how for morn their bosoms yearned,

   But pitying angels know ;

As restless, chilled and suffering,

They heard some far-off footstep ring,

   Or dismal water flow.

That night, O God ! how long it seemed,

   The moon how slow to set ;

The stars, all frozen where they beamed,

   At rising, lingering yet ;

One dead, dead sea of cold grey light,

No wavelet rippling o'er its white,

   Their aching vision met.

'T is morning on the battle field ;

   Chaunt low, ye lips of song !

Tread softly where the trumpet pealed

   Defiance to the strong ;

Nor question now these warriors bold,

With death's firm seal on lips so cold,
   If war be right or wrong?

A war horse, proud and sleek as glass,
   Obedient to the rein,
He softly climbed the mountain pass,
   Or dashed along the plain ;
He knew his master's kindly eye,
And rocked him like a lullaby,
   Or whirled him on amain.

But lo ! upon the morning's breath
   His nostrils gap and close ;
He struggles with the monster death,
   In faint, expiring throes.
A head is pillowed on his side—
Two fresh warm streams together glide—
   And on the crimson flows.

"Our Charlie" on this knoll of moss !—
   Sweet face and locks of brown—

One broad red line this brow across,

   The rest as soft as down;

A little hand is tightly pressed

Where throbbed a heart—a childish chest—

   And all as cold as stone.

Our farmer friend—with eyes of jet,

   Full face and raven locks—

We saw him clasp his "dear Jeanette!"

   And lingering view his flocks;

Ah! all but love in death was weak—

Tears cut the dust on either cheek

   Now bleaching on the rocks.

A slender frame—a thin sad face—

   Yet blood nor scar is here;

The sick man goaded in his place

   By "coward" uttered near,

Whose feverish pulse and aching head

For many a weary week had plead

   For home, but none would hear.

And lo! he fired a few poor rounds,
  With feeble hands astrain ;
Then heard no more the babel sounds
  That rocked the battle plain.
" Home, home " he whispered, " send me home "—
" Come home ! " God's angel answered, " come
  Where none shall mock thy pain."

Our village pet—the drummer lad—
  Who, with a joyous spring,
Went out to " see the troops parade,"
  And joined the martial ring.
Men won him—MEN ! unfeeling souls—
By flattery, to their muster rolls—
And here he lies—poor thing !

The Irish lad—good news that hailed
  From far Columbia's shore—
His mother blessed him, as he sailed
  The deep blue ocean o'er.
His neck yet wears the tiny cross

Upon a faded cord of floss

 His little sister wore.

" A little while ! a little while ! "

 Their grieving lips repeat,

As o'er the homestead's crumbling stile

 He clambers to the street—

" A little while ! my mother dear,

 I 'll send for ye another year—"

 Where will that trio meet ?

Who slumbers here ? the man that years

 Embrowed in glory's wreath—

Amid his country's deafening cheers

 He was enrolled by death.

But lo ! the white lamb of his flock

Hath met with him the fatal shock—

 Oh ! speak in underbreath !

A very child, whose lips and brow

 But " mother's " kiss had known,

As pulseless as a drift of snow,
  Beside the stalwart one ;
The cedar of the household shrine
Beside the bud—the fragile vine
  Left storm-tossed—all alone !

The sun is high. This red, red sea
  By living waves is stirred ;
They come from every mount and lea—
  The sick of hope deferred ;
" My father ! " " O, my child ! my child !"
" My brother ! " rings in anguish wild
  Where comes no answering word.

" My husband," comes in wailing tones
  From one whose years are few ;
" My only son ! " a mother moans,
  " I know these eyes of blue ! "
A father bowed with age and woe,
Up-lifts a forehead cold as snow,
  And wipes away its dew.

God help ye! one—and help ye all
    When hope's last spark dies out,
And, homeward bound, your footsteps fall
    Along the dismal route ;
Or, bearing hence your precious freight,
Ye ope again the homestead gate,
    And hang your weeds about.

Names too obscure for history,
    No marts contend your birth,
No statue rises where ye lie
    To point the world your worth.
Mute fibres in the arm of might,
Unknown ye blent in desperate fight,
    Unknown returned to earth.

But, rulers in imperial halls
    That wield a nation's rod,
" The private " answered to your calls,
    Obedient unto blood ;

A youth is rejoicing in manhood's light,

   And the strength of a sinewy frame;

The goal of his hopes is afar and bright,

   And he sighs for an honored name.

He patiently bends through the midnight hours

   Over pages of musty lore;

Not a cloud, as he sees, in his future lowers,

   All is rosy and bright before.

A husband is leading a beautiful bride

   To the home of his early years,

And a matron woman, with joy and pride,

   There blesses them both with tears.

But a little time, and that mother sleeps.

   In the church-yard, cold and low,

Where the summer smiles and the autumn weeps,

   All unknown in the city below.

Fair children have come to his yearning breast,

   And his cup of joy is full;

And he seeks to provide for his household nest,

    With a love that is beautiful !

But close to the grave where his mother lies,

    Is another green grave made ;

Another has closed her earthly eyes

    To awake in the realms of shade.

The laurels upon his brow are green,

    But he feels their tremor with pain ;

The loved of his youth has said " good e'en,"

    And her morning comes never again.

His children are roaming o'er land and sea,

    And have loves and homes afar ;

To the mammon of Gold they have bowed the knee,

    Or are led by Ambition's star.

The old man sits at his desolate hearth,

    Whence the fire is almost gone—

Not a cheerful song, nor a tone of mirth

    Is heard by the lonely one.

The night wind sweeps through the shivered pines,

And moans through the driving rain,

And whistles a tune in the skeleton vines

Of the time-worn window-pane.

He bends o'er his shadowy hearth, and grieves,

And wipes the cold sweat from his brow—

Hark! pattering feet 'neath the dripping eaves,

And his wife's sweet voice so low!

His absent children and buried wife

Come gliding in at the door—

The sea of death drinks the bubble Life

And he wakes on the unknown shore.

WYOMING.

Morning was rosy, beautiful and bright,
Mantling the hill-tops with a crown of light,
    Gilding the streams ;
Fast curling upward rolled the smoke away,
Light-hearted children waked, to shout and play,
    From pleasant dreams.

Lay God's own Volume open on the stand ;
Turning its pages with a reverent hand
    Sat the priest-sire ;
Welled the prayer upward from their hearts to **heaven,**
To the Great Father for the rest he'd given,
    For food and fire.

Hot lay the sun-beams on Wyoming's hills ;
Sparkled the bubbles on the clear, bright rills
    Over the river.

13

Walked the tree-shadow, as approached the noon ;

Chanted the river that low, gurgling tune,

Chanted forever.

Flitted the shadows lightly o'er the grain ;

Whistled the farmer, sauntering home again,

" Home, sweet home ; "

Sang the red-robin, in the tree-top high,

Plucking the cherries of his own July,

" Summer has come."

Smiling the matron to the door hath hied ;

" Rest thee, my husband, till the eventide,

Come in and rest ;

See ! Susquehannah glimmereth like glass,

Weary winged zephyrs scarcely stir the grass,

Fresh from the West.

" Sheltered, the robin trilleth now her song—

Rest thee, my husband, love, nor life is long ;

Toil not, I say ;

Bring thee, our daughter, cooling milk and bread,

Bring the ripe berries, and the cherries red,

    Gathered to-day."

Smiling, he thanks them, sitting in the door,

Prince in his cabin ; he, a serf before,

    Sad and afar.

Crowing, the baby to the chair creeps up,

Lifts he the darling ; shares the babe his cup,

    Lisping, " papa."

Hark : was it thunder ?   No cloud doth appear—

Hark !—'t is the war-hoop, the savage is near ;

    Grasps he the sword,

Shoulders the rifle, and murmurs " Farewell ! "

Louder the fireing, more dismal the yell—

    " Trust in the Lord."

Neighbors are arming, and fighting, and flying,

Mothers and children together are crying,

    Brother meets brother ;

Merciless brother, his brother to slay—
Born of one mother, and foeman to-day,
    Oh, God! of one mother!

Flashes the rifle, and whizzeth the ball,
Praying and cursing, together they fall,
    Weltering in gore;
Mothers and infants and beautiful girls—
Streams the red life-current fast thro' their curls,
    Over the floor.

Red rain is sprinkled o'er flower-bed and road,
Carnage is weary of terror and blood;
    Setteth the sun;
Chanteth the river a funeral hymn
Over the sleepers whose vision is dim,
    Whose life-work is done.

Comes in the West-wind, and plays with the hair
Of the baby that crept to its father's chair
    At the hot noon-tide;

Lingers around them a holy spell—
Mother and maiden and babe—'t is well—
    Thus a Holier died.

Flashes a light over midnight's brow ;
Cottage and field are consuming now ;
    Wyoming,
Ringeth thy hills with the orgies dire
Of the savage fiends o'er their midnight fire,
    As they dance and sing.

———

Poet, thy dreamings are not all ideal ;
Many a " Gertrude," living, loving, real,
    More sadly fell.
Oh ! day of terror, and oh, night of sorrow !
From fancy's realm we have no need to borrow,
    If truth we tell.

Time, with his bleak winds, hath the valley swept,
Sunshine has bleached them, and the clouds have wept
    The stains away ;

Haply the farmer here his grain doth gather,

Beauty and love dwell here again together,

    And Christians pray.

But until earth's last field is ploughed and sown,

Her last sheaf bound, the last green meadow mown,

    History will bring

Tales of the martyrs of the long ago—

Brave hearts, yet peaceful, as thy river's flow,

    Fair Wyoming!

HONOR OF LABOR.

You talk of the "honor of labor,"
   Looking down from your windows so high
On the sun-darkened brow of your neighbor,
   With a very benevolent eye ;
You tell him that "labor is noble,"
   As he turns the hard earth with his spade,
And wealth is a troublesome bauble,
   And fashions and titles will fade.

You stand in the glow of the forges,
   And talk of the iron and steam,
You sing of the snowy-winged barges
   Which flit o'er the main and the stream ;
You tell him his strength is Herculean,
   That the muscles stand out in his arm
Like the belts of the upper cerulean,
   Which border the skirts of the storm.

You praise his huge hand as he lifts it,

To fall in its terrible might ;

The ore waxing hard as he shifts it,

The stars waxing pale in the night ;

You talk of the steed never weary,

Which mocks at both rider and rein,

And bid him be patient and cheery,

Who *ironed* his path o'er the plain.

You call him your " friend " and your " brother,"

As you shrink from his touch with your glove,

And haste from that " hell " ere you smother,

Leaving him to wax cool with your love ;

You inhale the pure breeze, and are thankful

You can go when you please and can come ;

And count over your treasures, a bank full,

As you sit on your cushions at home.

Yes labor *is* honest and comely

To the drones which the honey devour,

But labor is care-worn, and homely
  To the bees which improve every hour;
And Labor oft feels in his pocket—
  He is fond of good "dinners" and "teas;"
And his patience goes off like a rocket,
  When he can't get a moment of ease.

Would you think of the "honor of labor"
  If your back like a rainbow were bent?
You'd forget your nobility—neighbor—
  When your landlord was clamoring for rent;
You'd forget the renown of the "order"
  Of labor's rag-liveried sons,
When the constable stepped o'er the border
  Of home, with his "writs" and his duns.

Labor thinks of his wife and his mother,
  How they tug at the needle and loom;
He longs, 'mid the clatter and smother
  Of the forge, for the pleasures of home;
13*

He thinks of the children that love him,

Untaught, and uncared for at times ;

And he hates the proud nabobs above him,

Who *pay him more flattery than dimes.*

DEACON HEZEKIAH.

O, Hezekiah 's a pious soul !

With his phiz as long as a hickory pole,

And he would n't smile if you 'd give him the whole

Of the gold in California ;

There he is, like a cloud, in his Sunday pew,

With his book in his hand, in his long-tailed blue,

And you 'd better take care or he 'll look you through,

With a glance that says, " I scorn you,"

He is very straight, and narrow, and tall,

From his crown to the hem of his overall ;

And he sings the psalm with a woeful drawl,

And a mouth like a clam's when it 's crying ;

But when Monday comes, he is up with the sun,

His *religion* is over, his work begun,

And you 'd think that there was n't a world but one,

And he had n't a thought of dying.

You would think he was sorry he'd lost a day,

As he rushes and rattles and drives away,

As he gives the poor orphan a crusty " nay,"

     And the widow a vinegar greeting ;

And he bargains, and sells, and collects his rent,

Nor tears nor petitions can make him relent,

Till he gets in his pocket each doubtful cent,

     Though he would 't *be seen* a cheating !

And Tuesday, and Wednesday, and all the week,

He does n't know Gentile, nor Jew, nor Greek,

Nor care whom he robs of the last beef-steak,

     Nor the last poor hope of fire ;

But Hezekiah is pious, very !

For who in the world ever saw him merry ?

And he looks as forlorn as a dromedary,

     And his voice, of itself, is a choir.

REV. JOHN ELLIOT PREACHING TO THE AMERICAN INDIANS.

No roof was o'er him but the arching sky,
 No floor beneath him but the swelling turf;
His temple pillars were the mountains high,
 His organ music was the sounding surf.

His calm eye rested on the low-browed squaws
 And shaven scalps that flecked the emerald sward,
While boldly taught he great Jehovah's laws,
 And told the story of our risen Lord.

Proud Sachems listened to the wondrous tale,
 And dusky maidens gave an eager ear ;
The stern lip quivered, and the cheek waxed pale
 That ne'er before was traversed by a tear.

Unselfish herald of the holy cross,

   Meek sufferer for His sake who died for all,

Uncounted ever was thy gain or loss,

   Resigned to linger, and prepared to fall.

To linger on in hunger, heat or cold,

   To toil for aye through weary nights and days,

If but one wanderer from his Master's fold

   Might be in-gathered to His lasting praise.

He did not seek the pomp and pride of earth,

   Nor yearned his spirit for the wreath of fame,

He deemed them all but poor and little worth,

   Weighed in the balance with eternal shame.

THE GREENHOUSE PLANT.

Into life the young leaves crept,
April smiled and April wept ;
 Then came May ;
Singing songs of love and mirth,
Spring went dancing o'er the earth,
 Blithe and gay ;
Saying : "Let your hearts be light,
Morn is pleasant, noon is bright,
 Care, good day."

Summer came with deeper bloom,
Brighter colors crossed her loom ;
 With liberal hand,
Strewed she blessings far and wide
Where so 'er the earth-born bide ;
 To every land

Walked she forth with stately tread,

Rainbows circling round her head,

Calm and bland.

Blossoms, purple, red and gold,

At her genial touch unfold;

Luscious fruit,

Tasseled corn and waving grain,

Greet the sunshine and the rain,

Where treads her foot;

All the sustenance of life,

All with shade or beauty rife,

Take form and root.

Change again o'er earth hath passed,

Graceful Summer goes at last,

With weary feet,

And a face of paler hue,

Gazing, pensive, on the blue.

In slow retreat,

Musing on the vines and flowers,

Death-doomed, lingering in her bowers,

    Frail and sweet.

Lo ! the grain is in the sheaves,

Ruder breezes sweep the leaves ;

    One by one

Fall they, rustling o'er the ground,

And we hear a wailing sound—

    Summer's gone ;

Autumn with a statelier mien,

Russet robe, and golden sheen,

    Fills her throne.

Regal Autumn bows to death ;

Winter comes with icy breath—

    King is he.

On he comes, with hail and rain

Rattling on the window-pane

    Merrily ;

Spreading snow-sheets on the hill,

Locking up the lake and rill,

    Ruthlessly.

Only one doth scorn his power,

She, a little fragile flower,

    A wee-bit thing;

Peeping from her house of glass,

Smiles to see the ruffian pass,

    Saying: " King!

Blow and whistle, storm and rant,

Catch me if you can—you can 't—

    I'm safe till Spring."

TO AN UNKNOWN FRIEND.

In vain for thy image with yearning I call;
Thou hast set for no portrait in memory's hall,
But the voice of thy spirit hath spoken to mine,
And I 've answered its meaning in whispers to thine.

I know not if thy forehead is white as the snow,
While thine eye, like the eagle's, is flashing below;
If thy locks like the midnight are swept by the wind,
If they 're silvered by time, or by agony thinned.

But I know that thy soul to its mission is true
As the seraph's that flits o'er the face of the blue;
And thy love-gifts are scattered, as globules of glass,
At the feet of the heartless, who crush them and pass.

For the lot of the gifted is on thee; to cling
To the hopes which are hollow as blossoms of spring,

Though a thousand betray thee, another to trust,
Till thy idols are numerous as atoms of dust.

The world hath dealt hardly, my brother, with thee ;
For an under-toned anguish hath spoken to me,
In the voice of thy harp-strings, which grieve as they wake,
And the heart which doth sweep them is ready to break.

As the mother bends over the babe while it sleeps,
As the lover bends over the loved one that weeps,
As the sister draws near to the brother, bereft
Of the dear one that slept in his bosom and left.

As affection bends over the bosom that's crossed
By the whirlwind of passions, to save it, ere lost,
I would soothe thy wrung spirit by sympathy's balm,
Till thy night-dreams are sweet, and thy day-dreams are calm.

For the kindred of spirit in spirit may meet,
Though the life-paths be severed which ring with their feet,
And the voice of thy soul may yet whisper to mine,
While I answer its meaning in whispers to thine.

DUSTY CALIFORNIA.

I sit in a dusty corner,
  Of a dusty, though dusted hotel,
And never felt folorner,
  With so dusty a story to tell.

I rise, with my arms akimbo,
  And gaze on the dusty street,
And under the dusty window
  Walk men with their dusty feet.

The dusty women are trailing
  Their skirts on the dusty way,
Their dusty flounces sailing
  O'er gaiters dusty and gray.

The dusty urchins are strolling
  Along to the dusty schools,

And dusty vehicles rolling,
    Are drafted by dusty mules.

The trees are dusty and sombre,
    The meadows like dusty straw;
The flowers in the garden yonder
    Are the dustiest ever I saw.

Dust, dust from the roof to the cellar
    From the church-steeple down to the pave;
There is nothing so white but it's yellow,
    And nothing so gay but it's grave.

Dust, dust over hillside and prairie,
    Dust, dust throughout Aprils and Junes,
With an August as hot as Sahara,
    And September winds hot as simoons.

If ever I see California
    From the veil of her dustiness free,
Of the absence of dust I 'll inform ye,
    And the things then apparent to me.

HOME TO THE SICK.

The invalid sits in a cushioned chair,
   In a richly furnished room ;
Through graceful drapery steals the air
   With its soft Æolian tune ;
White fingers have parted his raven locks,
   And smoothed them over his brow,
And the faithful nurse on tiptoe walks—
   What more could he have just now ?

The skillful physician comes smiling in,
   And pronounces the danger passed,
As he counts the beats in his wrist so thin,
   Saying : " Science has triumphed at last."
But the invalid thinks of that distant fold,
   Where friendship was never bought,
And the voice of the stranger sounds harsh and cold,
   For he knows that he loves him not.

He thinks of his mother, who, far away,
 Doth pray for her absent child,
Or his own sweet wife, who day by day
 Hath wept, till she 's almost wild.
And he turns with distaste from the morsel sweet,
 Which is brought by the nurse's hand,
And yearns for the hour when his weary feet
 May turn back to his native land.

Oh, the wildest paths of the wide, wide world,
 With our hurrying steps may ring ;
We may shout where a flag was never unfurled,
 The name of our country and king.
In classic groves we may proudly tread,
 And our home be the world as we roam ;
But when flutters the pulse and swims the head,
 We have but *one dear little home.*

www.ingramcontent.com/pod-product-compliance
Lightning Source LLC
Chambersburg PA
CBHW031409270326
41929CB00010BA/1384